THE BEST OF
sew simple
OVER 50 QUICK PROJECTS
MAGAZINE

PLUS
Must-Have
SEWING
TECHNIQUES

A LEISURE ARTS PUBLICATION

ready, set...sew!

Welcome to the world of simple sewing! With this treasury of the best of *Sew Simple* magazine's fresh projects and easy-to-follow instructions, you now have the freedom to express yourself. Even if you've never sewn a stitch, you'll learn the basic skills while creating polished projects that you'll be proud to flaunt. If you're a seasoned seamstress, you'll find tons of inspiration, along with dozens of irresistible ideas to customize your home and your look.

In light of our busy lives, *Sew Simple's* philosophy is that sewing should be just that—simple. Our step-by-step approach makes it easy for you to stitch unique and stylish clothing, home decor projects and gifts.

Find out how quickly you can revamp a room with a few signature touches. Look at your closet in a whole new way when you learn to make over your wardrobe in a snap. We also provide you with a handy guide of basic terms and techniques, so the answers to your questions are always just a few pages away.

Think of each project as a jumping-off point for creativity, as you choose fabrics, colors and details that show off your personal style. As the compliments roll in, nothing beats the feeling you get when you say, "I made it myself!"

Happy sewing!

BETH BRADLEY

●　●　●　●　●

THE BEST OF
sew simple
MAGAZINE

sewsimple.com

EDITOR, *SEW NEWS*: ELLEN MARCH
EDITOR: BETH BRADLEY
ASSISTANT EDITOR: BREANNE HIGHT
ART DIRECTOR: ANN INEZ HARDELL
DESIGNER: CLAUDIA DANIELS
PHOTOGRAPHY: JOE HANCOCK STUDIO–JOE HANCOCK,
JON ROSE & SCOTT WALLACE

CKMEDIA

CEO: WILL MARKS
CFO: RICH HYBNER
VP/GROUP PUBLISHER: DAVID O'NEIL
VP/EDITORIAL DIRECTOR: LIN SORENSON
VP/DIRECTOR OF EVENTS: PAULA KRAEMER
VP CONSUMER MARKETING: SUSAN DUBOIS
SR. PRODUCTION DIRECTOR: TERRY BOYER

LEISURE ARTS
the art of everyday living

EDITOR IN CHIEF: SUSAN WHITE SULLIVAN
SPECIAL PROJECTS DIRECTOR: SUSAN FRANTZ WILES
DIRECTOR OF DESIGNER RELATIONS: DEBRA NETTLES
SR. PREPRESS DIRECTOR: MARK HAWKINS
PUBLISHING SYSTEMS ADMINISTRATOR: BECKY RIDDLE
PUBLISHING SYSTEMS ASSISTANTS: CLINT HANSON,
JOHN ROSE & KEIJI YUMOTO

VP AND COO: TOM SIEBENMORGEN
DIRECTOR OF FINANCE AND
ADMINISTRATION: LATICIA MULL DITTRICH
VP SALES AND MARKETING: PAM STEBBINS
DIRECTOR OF SALES AND SERVICES: MARGARET REINOLD
VP OPERATIONS: JIM DITTRICH
COMPTROLLER, OPERATIONS: ROB THIEME
RETAIL CUSTOMER SERVICE MANAGER: STAN RAYNOR
PRINT PRODUCTION MANAGER: FRED F. PRUSS

The Best of Sew Simple Magazine is published by Leisure Arts, Inc., 5701 Ranch Drive, Little Rock, Arkansas 72223-9633. 501-868-8800. www.leisurearts.com.

Library of Congress Control Number: 2009925307
ISBN-13: 978-1-60140-614-9
ISBN-10: 1-60140-614-2

contents

retro apron

BY PAM ARCHER

WHIP UP SOME RETRO FUN with this cute apron featuring rickrack trim and contrasting waistband, ties and pockets. Just cut a few pattern pieces from a coordinating fabric to create a more individualized look to this fun project.

Finished length: 18″ from natural waist

instructions

All seams are ¼″ unless otherwise indicated.

1. Preshrink the fabrics and rickrack trim, and press them flat prior to cutting.

2. Cut the apron and bib from the main fabric following the pattern guidesheet.

3. Fold the contrasting fabric in half lengthwise, aligning the cut edges. On the crosswise grain, cut the waistband, waist ties, neck ties and pockets (**A**).

4. Cut the interfacing as directed on the pattern guidesheet for the waistband and pockets.

5. Construct the apron following the pattern guidesheet.

YOU WILL NEED:

- Kwik Sew pattern 3320, view C, or similar pattern
- 1⅛ yards of 45″-wide fabric or ⅞ yard of 60″-wide fabric for apron body
- ¾ yard of 45″-wide fabric for contrast waist and neck ties and patch pockets
- ¼ yard of 24″-wide fusible interfacing
- 3½ yards of medium rickrack
- matching thread for main fabric
- matching thread for rickrack
- 70/10 or 80/12 sewing machine needle
- press cloth

COLOR CUES

When adding a coordinating fabric to a sewing project, look to the main fabric for color clues. Study the colors used in the print or background for compatible companions that will give a balanced and attractive look.

Pull out several fabrics, along with the trim, and lay them together. Stand back and review the selections, checking for an overall harmonious look. If something seems too strong, try a softer color. Or if things seem a little blah, add a dash of bright trim, as featured on this project. The goal is to create an apron that looks as great as it makes you feel.

A Contrast Fabric Crosswise Layout

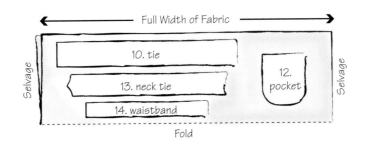

On the edge

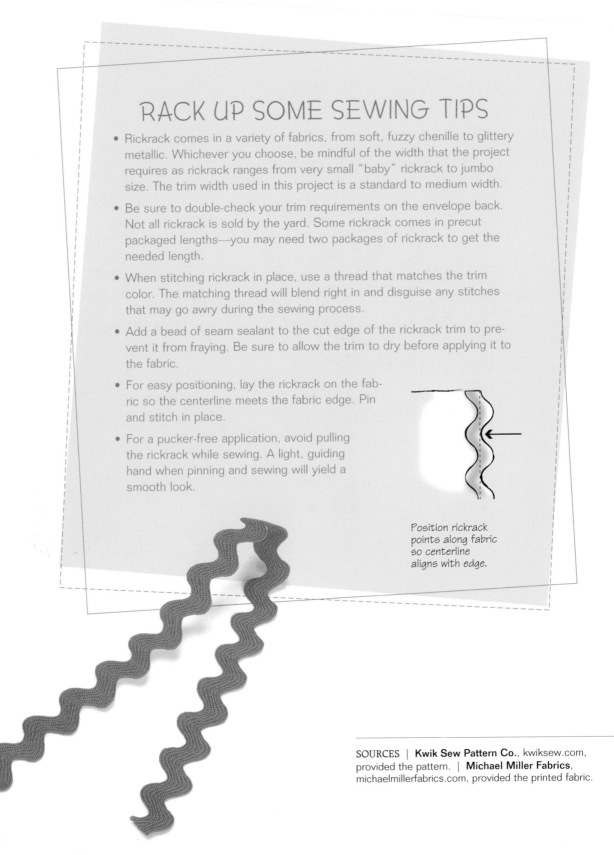

RACK UP SOME SEWING TIPS

- Rickrack comes in a variety of fabrics, from soft, fuzzy chenille to glittery metallic. Whichever you choose, be mindful of the width that the project requires as rickrack ranges from very small "baby" rickrack to jumbo size. The trim width used in this project is a standard to medium width.

- Be sure to double-check your trim requirements on the envelope back. Not all rickrack is sold by the yard. Some rickrack comes in precut packaged lengths—you may need two packages of rickrack to get the needed length.

- When stitching rickrack in place, use a thread that matches the trim color. The matching thread will blend right in and disguise any stitches that may go awry during the sewing process.

- Add a bead of seam sealant to the cut edge of the rickrack trim to prevent it from fraying. Be sure to allow the trim to dry before applying it to the fabric.

- For easy positioning, lay the rickrack on the fabric so the centerline meets the fabric edge. Pin and stitch in place.

- For a pucker-free application, avoid pulling the rickrack while sewing. A light, guiding hand when pinning and sewing will yield a smooth look.

Position rickrack points along fabric so centerline aligns with edge.

SOURCES | **Kwik Sew Pattern Co.**, kwiksew.com, provided the pattern. | **Michael Miller Fabrics**, michaelmillerfabrics.com, provided the printed fabric.

patchwork potholders

BY LINDA PERMANN

BY LINDA PERMANN

THESE CHEERFUL POTHOLDERS are the perfect renovation for a tired kitchen. Plus you can use your scraps and finish them in an afternoon—no contractor would be able to compete!

For your own safety, be sure to use at least one layer of heat-proof batting, such as Insul-Bright batting, which is heat resistant up to 400 degrees. Test the potholders before handling anything heated to a higher temperature.

instructions

Use ¼" seam allowances unless otherwise noted.

1. For each potholder, cut the following pieces, varying the fabrics used as desired: two 4¾" squares, one 1" x 9" strip, one 1½" x 9" strip, one 3¾" strip, one 9" square (backing) and one 2" x 7" strip (hanging loop).

2. Right sides facing, stitch the two 4¾" squares together along one edge. Press the seam to one side. Right sides facing, stitch the 1" x 9" strip to one long edge of the pieced squares. Press. Right sides facing, stitch the 1½"-wide strip to the 1"-wide strip; press. Right sides facing, stitch the 3¾"-wide strip to the 1½"-wide strip (**A**). Press, making sure that all seams point in the same direction. Repeat for the second potholder.

3. To make the hanging loop, fold one long edge of the 2" x 7" strip ½" toward the wrong side; press. Repeat with the other long edge. Fold the strip in half lengthwise; press. Stitch along the strip open edge (**B**).

Stitch along seams to quilt the potholder.

YOU WILL NEED:

(makes two 8"-square potholders)

- two 9" squares of Insul-Bright Batting
- two 9" squares of cotton batting (polyester might melt)
- assorted fat quarters or fabric remnants
- matching all-purpose thread
- quilting needle
- point turner

A Stitch fabric pieces.

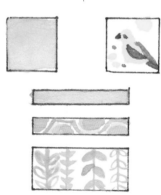

B Stitch along open edge.

4. Layer the pieces as follows: cotton batting, Insul-Bright batting, patchwork square (right side up), backing square (wrong side up). Fold the hanging loop in half; position it between the two fabric layers slightly to the right of one corner, aligning the raw edges (**C**). Pin the layers in place. Starting about 1″ from the left side, stitch around three edges and continue about 1″ into the fourth edge.

5. Carefully clip both batting squares as close to the stitching line as possible. Clip the corners. Turn the potholder right side out and use the point turner to smooth the corners. Press. Turn in the opening edges, clipping the batting if necessary to achieve a smooth seam; pin. Stitch around the entire potholder perimeter.

6. With the pieced side facing up, stitch across the horizontal lines just above seams.

Stitch one line down the potholder center slightly to the left of the pieced squares seam (**D**).

SOURCE | **Repropdepot.com** provided the fabric and Insul-Bright batting.

what's cookin'?

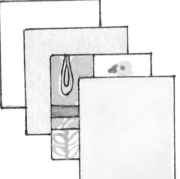

C Layer pieces.

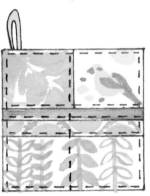

D Stitch along seams.

gathered apron

BY LINDA TURNER GRIEPENTROG

MASTER THE TECHNIQUE OF GATHERING (see page 182) while creating a funky apron. Pair it with the matching oven mitt on page 12, and prepare to wow your guests at your next party. Or, just throw it on when cooking a weekday meal to spice things up a bit.

instructions

1. Trim the selvage edges from the fabric, and cut a 22″ x 44″ rectangle.

2. Right sides together, fold the fabric in half widthwise. Position a round object, such as a dinner plate, on the lower corner. To round the lower corners, trace around part of the plate with a fabric-marking pen (**A**). Cut along the line.

3. Zigzag-finish the fabric edges.

4. Press under the rounded edge ½″. With the apron right side up, pin the trim under the pressed edge. Stitch in place (**B**).

5. Gather the straight edge to 18″. See "To Gather a Small Area" on page 183 for instructions.

6. Pin-mark the center of the gathered edge. Fold the ribbon in half widthwise to find the center; mark with a pin.

7. Position the ribbon over the gathered apron edge, matching the pins. Pin the ribbon in place, distributing the gathers evenly. Stitch along the ribbon lower edge and again down the center (**C**). Remove any exposed gathering threads.

8. Trim the ribbon ends at an angle, and apply seam sealant if desired to prevent fraying.

SOURCE | **Michael Miller Fabrics,**
michaelmillerfabrics.com, provided the fabric.

YOU WILL NEED:

• ⅝ yard of 45″-wide fabric

• 2 yards of coordinating 1″-wide grosgrain ribbon

• 1¼ yards of trim

• matching all-purpose thread

• fabric-marking pen

• seam sealant (optional)

A Trace around plate to round corners.

Fold

B Stitch trim in place.

C Stitch ribbon in place.

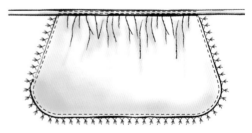

Tie a brown ribbon

oven mitt

BY AMY STALP

EVERY STYLISH CHEF NEEDS GOOD TOOLS. Why not start with an oven mitt that's as hot as the food you're serving? Even if the most gourmet thing you ever cook is a frozen pizza, you'll still look great taking it out of the oven. Add the apron from page 10, and you've got a matching set!

instructions

1. Cut two 9½" x 12" rectangles each from the main fabric, lining fabric and batting.

2. Place one lining fabric rectangle wrong side up on your work surface. Place one batting rectangle on the lining. Place one main fabric rectangle right side up on the batting. Pin around the edges. Repeat with the remaining rectangles.

3. To machine quilt each rectangle, mark vertical lines 1½" apart; stitch. Mark horizontal lines 1½" apart; stitch to form a grid (**A**). Repeat to quilt the second rectangle.

4. Photocopy the oven mitt pattern on page 15. Place the pattern on one quilted rectangle, and trace around the edges. Turn over the pattern and trace it on the second rectangle (**B**). Cut out the patterns.

YOU WILL NEED:

- ¼ yard of main fabric
- ¼ yard of lining fabric
- ¼ yard of batting
- medium rickrack trim
- matching all-purpose thread

If your fabric has a linear design, follow the lines in the pattern when quilting.

A Machine quilt rectangle.

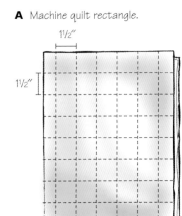

1½"

1½"

B Trace patterns.

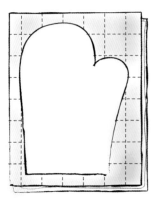

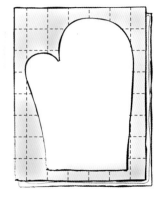

To make this project even faster, use pre-quilted fabric. Find it in fabric stores in a variety of colors and prints.

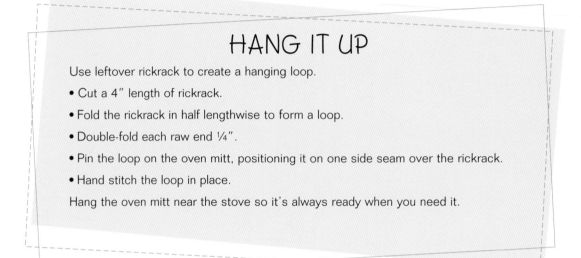

HANG IT UP

Use leftover rickrack to create a hanging loop.

- Cut a 4″ length of rickrack.
- Fold the rickrack in half lengthwise to form a loop.
- Double-fold each raw end ¼″.
- Pin the loop on the oven mitt, positioning it on one side seam over the rickrack.
- Hand stitch the loop in place.

Hang the oven mitt near the stove so it's always ready when you need it.

Rickrack is sold in precut lengths. One package of rickrack is more than enough for the oven mitt—you'll have plenty left over to embellish other projects.

5. Right sides together, stitch around the mitt using a ¼″ seam, leaving the lower edge free. Clip the inner thumb and around the curves, being careful not to cut through the stitching (**C**).

6. Turn up the lower edge ¼″; press. Turn up the edge ¼″ again; press. Stitch (**D**).

7. Turn the mitt right side out. Cut a length of rickrack long enough to fit around the lower edge, plus ½″ extra (approximately 12″).

8. Pin the rickrack around the lower edge, tucking under the raw ends. Stitch the rickrack in place (**E**).

SOURCE | **Michael Miller Fabrics,** michaelmillerfabrics.com, provided the main fabric.

C Stitch and clip mitt.

D Turn up lower edge; stitch.

E Stitch rickrack in place.

Oven Mitt Pattern

Cut 2 from fabric.
Cut 2 from lining.
Cut 2 from batting.

kitchen towels

BY AMY STALP

WHY SETTLE FOR PLAIN KITCHEN TOWELS when you can have fabulous ones? Spice up a simple set of towels with colorful fabric bands and charming hand embroidery. Use the same fabric for all four towels, or mix and match different colors and prints.

YOU WILL NEED:

(makes four towels)

- four 100% cotton tea towels

- ¼ yard each of four different 100% cotton fabrics or 1 yard of one fabric

- matching all-purpose thread

- embroidery floss

- embroidery needle and hoop

● ● ● ● ●

instructions

1. Preshrink the towels and fabrics.

2. Cut four fabric strips 5″ x the width of the towel plus 1″ for seam allowances.

3. Fold under ½″ on each long edge of one fabric strip; press. Fold under ½″ on each short edge; press.

4. Right side up, position the fabric strip on the lower edge of one towel; edgestitch in place (**A**).

5. With an air-soluble pen, write a word, draw or trace a picture, or trace around an object such as a cookie cutter.

6. Hoop, then hand stitch over the lines with two strands of embroidery floss, using a backstitch. Embellish with French knots, lazy daisy stitches or cross-stitches as desired. (See page 198 for hand embroidery stitches.)

7. Press the towel from the wrong side to remove any hoop marks.

8. Repeat for the three remaining towels.

SOURCE | **FreeSpirit Fabric,** freespiritfabric.com, provided the fabric.

A Stitch fabric in place.

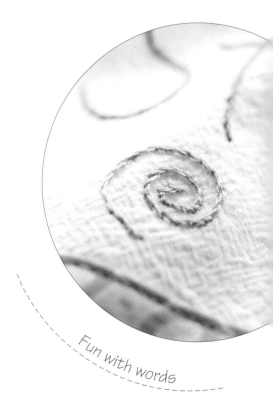

Fun with words

chair back slipcover

BY ELLEN MARCH

CHANGING YOUR DINING DÉCOR is as simple as picking out fabric. Choose a fancy fabric, such as silk doupioni or embroidered satin, and throw a dinner party to show off your new digs.

instructions

1. Measure the chair-back width and height (**A**). From the fabric, cut a rectangle the width plus 1″ by twice the height plus 1″. The featured chair measured 16¾″ x 19½″, so the fabric rectangle measured 17¾″ x 40″.

2. With wrong sides facing, fold the fabric in half widthwise. Press the fold using an appropriate heat setting for the fabric.

3. Stitch the side edges using ½″ seam allowances (**B**); press open the seams.

4. Fold the lower raw edge ¼″ to the wrong side; press. Fold again ¼″ to the wrong side; press. Stitch close to the second fold (**C**). Turn the cover right side out.

5. Repeat to create a second chair cover.

YOU WILL NEED:

(makes two chair covers)

- 2 yards of fabric (yardage may vary depending on chair)
- matching all-purpose thread

● ● ● ● ●

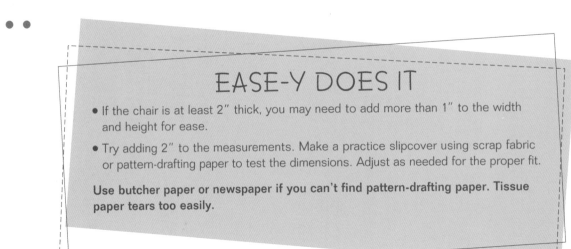

EASE-Y DOES IT

- If the chair is at least 2″ thick, you may need to add more than 1″ to the width and height for ease.
- Try adding 2″ to the measurements. Make a practice slipcover using scrap fabric or pattern-drafting paper to test the dimensions. Adjust as needed for the proper fit.

Use butcher paper or newspaper if you can't find pattern-drafting paper. Tissue paper tears too easily.

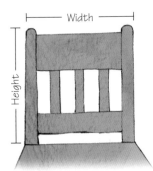

A Measure chair back.

Width

Height

B Stitch side edges.

Fold

C Stitch lower edge.

ON THE CURVE

If your chairs have curved backs, it's easy to make the covers hug the curves.

1. Place a large piece of paper on the floor or a flat work surface. Lay the chair down on the paper. Trace around the chair back (**1**).

2. Draw a line 1″ outside the traced line; cut along this line to form a pattern for the cover.

3. Use the pattern to cut two covers from the fabric. Zigzag- or serge-finish the curved edge on each cover.

4. Right sides facing, pin the covers together over the chair back. Pin-mark the widest part of the chair on each side. Make sure you can easily remove the cover. Using a ½″ seam, stitch around the cover between the pin marks, leaving the lower edge open (**2**).

5. On the unstitched portions of the curved edge, turn under ½″ to the wrong side; press. Stitch close to the folds.

6. Complete the cover as directed in step #4.

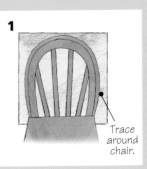

1

Trace around chair.

2

chair seat cover

BY ELLEN MARCH

ARE YOUR DINING ROOM CHAIRS IN NEED OF A NEW LOOK? Revamp your décor easily by making new chair covers to hide unsightly stains or outdated fabric—or to give the room a refreshing change of pace.

YOU WILL NEED:

(makes two chair covers)

• fabric (See steps #1-7 to determine the amount. The featured covers required 2 yards.)

• mediumweight interfacing (See steps #1-7 to determine the amount. The featured covers required 2 yards.)

• pattern-tracing cloth

• matching all-purpose thread

• air- or water-soluble fabric-marking pen

instructions

All seams are ½″ unless otherwise indicated.

1. Record the following chair seat measurements: seat length, seat-back width, seat-front width and seat drop (from the top of the seat cushion to 1″ below the seat depth) (**A**).

2. With an air- or water-soluble marking pen, draw the seat dimensions on the pattern-tracing cloth (**B**). Fold the pattern-tracing cloth in half lengthwise to check for symmetry. Adjust the markings if needed. Place the pattern-tracing cloth over the seat to make sure the markings align with the seat dimensions. Make additional adjustments if needed.

3. Draw a line ½″ around the drop measurement; cut out the seat pattern along the mark (**C**).

4. Place the pattern over the seat. Pin-fit the pattern to the seat at the front corners, creating a box shape; mark the back leg placements using the air-or water-soluble marking pen (**D**). Remove the pattern from the seat.

5. Cut off the excess pattern-tracing cloth at the front corners, leaving ½″ beyond the pins. Remove the pins.

A Measure chair seat.

A Seat length

B Seat-back width

C Seat-front width

D Drop (from top of seat cushion to 1″ below seat depth)

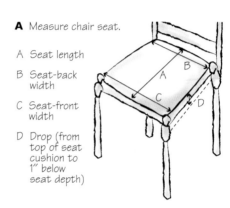

B Draw seat dimensions on pattern-tracing cloth.

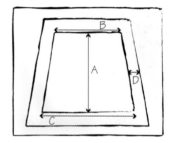

C Cut out pattern.

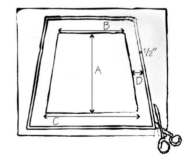

D Pin-fit pattern and mark back chair leg placements.

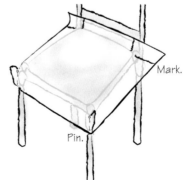

Mark.

Pin.

Since the chair covers are completely reversible, you can use different fabrics for each side and change your décor with a quick flip.

6. Draw a line ½" outside each chair back leg placement mark, stopping 1" from the inside corners. Using a CD or small plate as a guide, join each leg placement mark by drawing a curved line up to, but not touching, the original seat dimension markings. Cut along the marks (**E**).

7. Place the pattern over the seat to check the fit. Make adjustments if needed.

8. Use the pattern to cut four chair covers each from the fabric and interfacing. Fuse each interfacing piece to each chair cover wrong side, following the manufacturer's instructions.

9. Cut eight 1½"x 22 ½" strips from the fabric. Right sides together, fold each strip in half lengthwise; press. Stitch one short end and the long raw edge of each fabric strip. Turn the strips right side out; press.

10. Right sides together, stitch the front corners of each chair cover (**F**). Press the seams open. On one chair cover right side, pin four strap raw ends to adjacent chair back leg flaps 1½" from the inside corners (**G**). Repeat to pin the remaining straps to a second chair cover.

11. Place one pinned chair cover inside an unpinned chair cover, right sides facing; align the corner seams. Move the straps away from the stitching area to avoid stitching over them in the next step. Stitch around the chair covers, removing the pins as you stitch over the straps. Leave a 4" opening along one side edge for turning.

12. Turn the chair cover right side out; press, folding in the opening raw edges. Topstitch around the chair cover, closing the opening with the stitches. Repeat to sew the remaining chair cover.

SOURCE | **Quilt Gallery**, (406) 257-5799, quiltgallery.net, provided the fabric.

E Cut along leg placement marks.

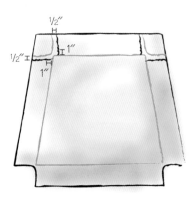

F Stitch front corners.

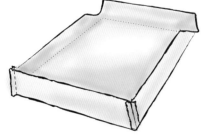

G Pin strap raw ends to chair cover.

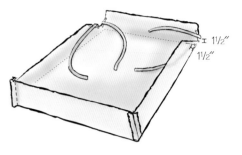

A good fit

reversible coasters

BY AMY STALP

CLASS UP YOUR NEXT GATHERING with an elegant set of reversible coasters. Contrasting thread and a built-in decorative stitch are all you need to add just the right touch of subtle embellishment. The coasters are the perfect addition to a party, whether you're entertaining a crowd or just a few friends.

instructions

Use ½″ seam allowances unless otherwise noted.

1. From fabric A cut four 5½″ squares.

2. From fabric B cut four 5½″ squares.

3. Right sides facing, stitch one fabric A and one fabric B square together, leaving an opening along one edge for turning (**A**).

4. Clip the corners and turn the coaster right side out.

5. Press the coaster, turning in the opening edges. Slipstitch the opening closed.

6. Using a ruler and a fabric-marking pen, draw a line ½″ from one edge. Draw two more lines, spacing each ½″ apart.

7. Select a decorative stitch on the sewing machine. Stitch along the center line.

8. Straight stitch along the two outer lines (**B**).

9. Using a ruler and a fabric-marking pen, draw a line ½″ from one edge and perpendicular to the stitched lines. Draw two more lines, spacing each ½″ apart.

10. Stitch along the lines as directed in steps #7 and #8 (**C**).

11. Repeat to make three more coasters.

YOU WILL NEED:

(makes four coasters)

- ¼ yard or a fat quarter of fabric A
- ¼ yard or a fat quarter of fabric B
- ruler
- fabric-marking pen
- contrasting all-purpose thread
- hand-sewing needle

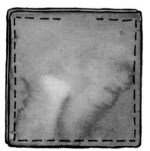

A Stitch around square, leaving opening for turning.

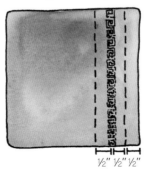

B Add decorative and straight stitching.

½″ ½″ ½″

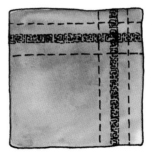

C Stitch perpendicular to first lines.

SEWING CIRCLE

Bright fabrics and circle appliqués create a completely different, more casual coaster. Stitching the circles helps you perfect your pivoting technique. To make this project easier, use triangle or square appliqués.

instructions

Use ½" seam allowances unless otherwise noted.

YOU WILL NEED:

(makes four coasters)

- ⅓ yard of fabric A

- scraps of four other fabrics

- all-purpose thread matched to fabric A

1. From fabric A cut eight 5½" squares.

2. Cut four 2"-diameter circles from each of the four fabric scraps.

3. Position one of each colored circle over a fabric A square, slightly overlapping the circles. Use a fabric-marking pen to trace around each circle. Remove the circles.

4. Position one circle on the fabric A square right side. Straight stitch around the circle (**1**).

5. Position a second circle over the coaster, slightly overlapping the first. Stitch (**2**).

6. Repeat to stitch the two remaining circles (**3**).

7. Repeat to stitch circles on three more fabric A squares.

8. Right sides facing, stitch a plain square and a stitched square together, leaving an opening for turning.

9. Clip the corners. Turn the coaster right side out.

10. Press the coaster, turning in the opening edges. Slipstitch the opening closed.

11. Repeat to stitch three more coasters.

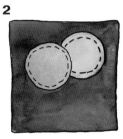

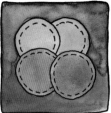

framed place mat

BY DONNA BABYLON

FACING ANOTHER HUM-DRUM DAY at the office or a heavy class schedule is a lot easier when your morning table is set with colorful and cheery place mats. They're easy to make, so you can stitch up a matching set in no time.

instructions

Finished size: 13" x 20"

1. Cut two 17" x 24" rectangles from the backing fabric. Cut two 12¾" x 19¾" rectangles each from the batting and center fabric.

2. On one 17" x 24" rectangle, fold under 1" toward the wrong side on each lengthwise edge;

press. Turn under each edge 1" again; press (**A**). Repeat to double fold and press the rectangle side edges.

3. Unfold the fabric at one corner. To miter the corner, diagonally fold the corner toward the wrong side where the inner foldlines intersect; press (**B**). Unfold the fabric.

Mitered corners are easy to create with a few folds.

YOU WILL NEED:

(makes two place mats)

- ¾ yard of fabric (backing & border)

- ⅝ yard of fabric (center)

- ⅝ yard of low-loft fleece-type batting

- all-purpose thread to match backing fabric

As another option, use solid fabric for the center and embellish it with hand embroidery or decorative stitching.

A Double fold lengthwise edges.

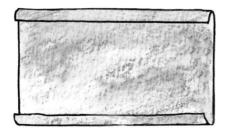

B Fold corner.

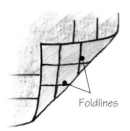

Foldlines

BATTING

Batting is the soft layer that goes between the top and the backing of a project (such as a quilt, wall hanging, place mat or garment). Batting adds dimension and definition.

Batting comes in different thicknesses (or lofts) and fibers, such as cotton and polyester. Purchase batting by the yard or in prepackaged sizes.

4. Fold the fabric where the outer foldlines intersect; press. Cut the fabric along this foldline (**C**).

5. Refold the rectangle edges, keeping the corner fabric tucked inside. The edges will meet at a 45° angle to form a mitered corner (**D**).

6. Repeat to miter the remaining three corners.

7. Unfold the rectangle edges. Position the batting within the inner foldlines. Right side up, position the center fabric rectangle over the batting. Refold the edges over the center fabric; pin in place.

8. Stitch along the border inner edge through all layers (**E**). Hand stitch the diagonal folds of each mitered corner together (**F**).

9. Repeat to stitch the second place mat.

C Fold and cut corner.

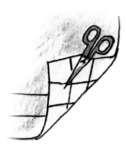

D Fold edges to form mitered corner.

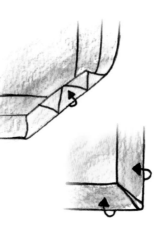

E Stitch border.

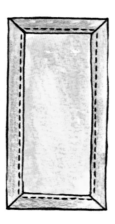

F Hand stitch corner.

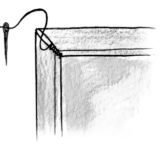

table runner

BY AMY STALP

EVEN SITTING DOWN FOR A BOWL OF CEREAL will seem like a special occasion when you set your table with this luxurious silk table runner. The rich colors and silver bangles will cast a radiant glow over your meal, whether you're entertaining a crowd or hosting an intimate gathering for friends.

instructions

Stitch all seams right sides together with a ½" seam allowance unless otherwise indicated. Press all seams open.

Finished size: approximately 13"x54"

1. From the purple silk, cut two 14"x28" rectangles, one 7"x14" rectangle, four 6"x14" rectangles and two 4"x14" rectangles.

2. From the lime green silk, cut two 6"x14" rectangles and six 2"x14" rectangles.

3. From the turquoise silk, cut two 3"x14" rectangles and two 2"x14" rectangles.

4. Sort the strips into groups (**A**). Sew the strips of each group together along the lengthwise edges.

5. Arrange the strip groups as shown; stitch (**B**).

6. To create the backing, stitch the two 14"x28" purple rectangles together at one short end.

7. Cut the trim in half. Lay the table runner top right side up on a flat surface. Place one trim length along each short edge, aligning the trim

> Use a zipper foot to stitch the beaded trim in place— the narrow foot makes it easier to navigate around the beads.

YOU WILL NEED:

- ⅞ yard of purple silk
- ¼ yard of lime green silk
- ¼ yard of turquoise silk
- ⅞ yard of beaded trim
- thread: matching all-purpose, silver metallic

A Separate strips into groups.

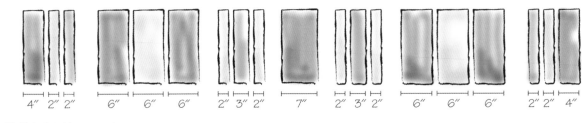

4" 2" 2"   6" 6" 6"   2" 3" 2"   7"   2" 3" 2"   6" 6" 6"   2" 2" 4"

B Stitch table runner top.

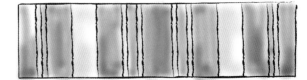

header (the flat section that the beads are attached to) with the fabric edge. Stitch along the header (**C**).

8. Matching the raw edges, stitch the table runner top to the backing rectangle, leaving a 6″ opening for turning along one long edge. Push the beads away from the stitching area as you sew. Clip the corners, and turn the table runner right side out; press.

9. Set up the machine with silver metallic thread in the needle and purple thread in the bobbin.

10. With the pieced side up, edgestitch around the table runner, closing the opening with the stitches.

11. Quilt the table runner along the vertical seams. Stitch in the ditch along each seam, or use a decorative stitch (**D**). For a unique look, alternate between stitching in the ditch and decorative stitching.

Alternate between stitching in the ditch and decorative stitching.

SOURCE | **Exotic/Thai Silks,** thaisilks.com, provided the 54″-wide silk doupioni in colors #406 (lime green), #455 (turquoise) and #309 (purple).

Experiment with different fabric and trim combinations. For example, using cotton fabric results in a much more casual look.

C Stitch trim to top.

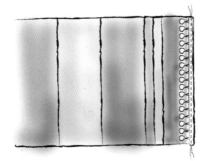

D Quilt the table runner.

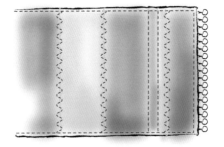

special occasion napkins

BY AMY STALP

WHEN YOU'RE SETTING THE TABLE FOR A HOLIDAY OR SPECIAL OCCASION, make the napkins part of the decorations with simple hand embroidery.

instructions

1. Place one napkin right side up on your working surface. Use the fabric marking pen to write a message around one corner. Tailor the message to the occasion, such as Happy Birthday, Merry Christmas, the couple's names for an anniversary, etc.

2. Using two strands of embroidery floss, stitch over the drawn letters using a backstitch.

3. Using three strands of the other color embroidery floss, make a French knot on both sides of each word. See page 198 for hand embroidery instructions.

4. Repeat for each napkin, alternating embroidery floss colors.

YOU WILL NEED:

• napkins

• 2 colors of embroidery floss

• hand-sewing needle

• fabric marking pencil

● ● ● ● ●

napkin rings and napkins

BY ELLEN MARCH

A SMALL PROJECT, SUCH AS A NAPKIN RING, is a great way to boost your confidence when sewing with leather. Of course, you can always choose a favorite cotton print or corduroy instead to compliment your table décor however you wish.

instructions

Use ¼" seams unless otherwise noted.

YOU WILL NEED:

(makes four napkin rings)

- ⅛ yard of faux leather
- four ¾"-diameter buttons
- size 16/100 leather-sewing needle
- air-soluble fabric-marking pen
- hand-sewing needle
- matching all-purpose thread

● ● ● ● ● ●

1. From the leather, cut eight 3½" x 10" rectangles.

2. With two rectangles right sides facing stitch around the rectangle perimeter, leaving a 4" opening along the lower edge for turning (choose one long edge as the lower edge) (**A**).

3. Turn the napkin ring right side out through the opening. Use a knitting needle or chopstick to

PINKY RING

If turning layers of leather right side out and decorative stitching through bulky seams isn't for you, here's another option.

1. Position two leather rectangles wrong sides together. Straight stitch around the perimeter ¼" from the edges.

2. Use pinking shears to pink the seam allowance close to the stitching.

3. Stitch the buttonhole and button as directed on page 36.

For slip-free sewing, use spray adhesive to secure the rectangles with wrong sides together.

A Stitch around perimeter.

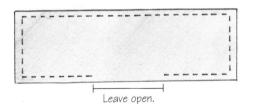

Leave open.

See page 193 for more leather-sewing tips and advice

push out the corners. Finger-press the seams and fold in the opening raw edges. Clip the opening closed using a binder clip or paper clip (**B**).

4. Select a decorative stitch on your machine, or select a narrow zigzag stitch. Stitch ¼″ inside the napkin-ring perimeter (**C**), closing the opening with the stitches and removing the binder clip as you sew.

5. Using an air-soluble marking pen, draw a 1″-long vertical line centered ½″ from one napkin-ring end (**D**). Stitch a 1″-long buttonhole along the mark.

6. Roll the napkin ring around your fingers so the buttonhole end overlaps the opposite end by 1½″. Mark the button placement (**E**). Unfold the napkin ring and sew the button in place by hand.

7. Repeat to create three more napkin rings.

Consult the sewing machine manual to learn how to stitch an automatic button-hole. This streamlines your sewing and allows you to stitch all four buttonholes with ease.

B Clip opening closed.

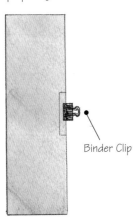

Binder Clip

C Decorative stitch perimeter.

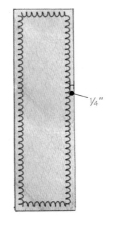

¼″

D Mark buttonhole.

1″ ½″

E Mark button placement.

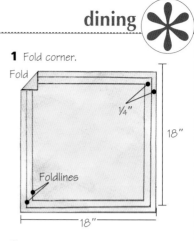
NAPKINS

Make napkins to coordinate with your new napkin rings. All you need is some cute fabric!

YOU WILL NEED

(makes one napkin)

- one 18½" square of fabric
- matching or contrasting thread

instructions

1. Double fold each fabric edge ¼" toward the wrong side; press. Unfold the edges.

2. Fold one corner so the tip overlaps the second foldline (**1**); press. Repeat to fold each corner.

3. Refold all edges along the previous foldlines so each corner is concealed. Re-press if needed.

4. Straight stitch around the napkin perimeter along the inner fold (**2**).

5. Optional: Slipstitch each corner intersection closed.

1 Fold corner.

2 Straight stitch perimeter.

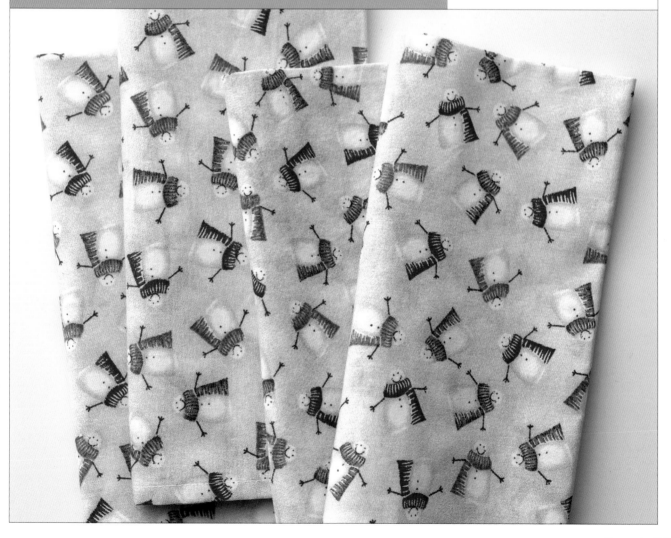

outdoor table setting

BY DEBBIE HOMER

MAKE A CHEERY AND PRACTICAL SUMMER TABLE SETTING USING OUTDOOR FABRIC. Outdoor fabric, such as Sunbrella, works well because it's substantial; washable; fast drying; and stain-, fade- and mildew-resistant. Cute pockets keep napkins and plastic utensils from blowing away on a breezy day.

place mat

instructions

Use ½" seam allowances unless otherwise noted.

1. Wrong sides facing, position the 14"x20" fabric rectangle over the 17"x23" fabric rectangle so that there's 1½" of backing around each place mat outer edge.

2. Fold one backing long edge 1½" over one place mat long edge. Fold the backing folded corner at a 45° angle (**A**). Fold the backing short edge over the place mat to create a mitered-corner effect; pin. Repeat for the other three corners.

3. Overcast stitch around the backing raw edges and diagonally along the folded mitered-corner edges. Finger-press.

4. Right sides facing, fold the 6½"x9" fabric rectangle in half lengthwise. Designate one short edge as the lower edge. Mark the open long edge 2" up from the lower edge. Draw a diagonal line connecting the mark to the lower folded edge. With the rectangle still folded, cut along the line.

5. Fold the pocket upper edge 2" toward the fabric right side; finger-press. Overcast stitch across the raw short edge.

6. Position the pocket right side up over the place mat right side. Position the pocket lower point and right side edge ¼" from the backing lower and right overcast edges; pin (**B**).

7. Overcast stitch around the pocket side and lower edges.

A Fold backing over place mat.

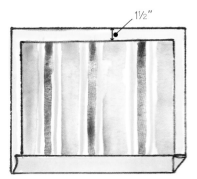

1½"

B Position pocket on place mat; pin.

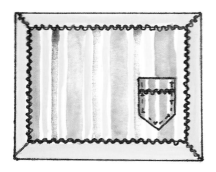

TABLE RUNNER

Finished size
14"x60"

- two 15"x61"
  rectangles of
  orange outdoor
  fabric

- two 7½"x12"
  rectangles of lime-
  green-and-white
  striped outdoor
  fabric (pockets)

- all-purpose lime
  green thread

- scissors or
  rotary cutter

- air-soluble fabric
  marking pen

table runner

instructions

Use ½" seam allowances unless otherwise noted.

1. Right sides facing, fold one 15"x61" rectangle in half lengthwise. Designate one short edge as the lower edge. Mark the open long edge 6" up from the lower edge. Draw a diagonal line connecting the mark to the lower folded edge (**C**).

2. With the fabric still folded, cut along the line. Repeat for the other short end and for the other 15"x61" fabric rectangle short ends.

3. Right sides facing, fold one 7½"x12" fabric rectangle in half lengthwise. Designate one short edge as the lower edge. Mark the open long edge 3" up from the lower edge. Draw a diagonal line connecting the mark to the lower folded edge. With the rectangle still folded, cut along the line. Repeat for the other 7½"x12" fabric rectangle.

4. Fold one pocket upper edge 3" toward the fabric right side; finger-press. Set the machine for an overcast stitch. Stitch across the raw short edge (**D**). Repeat to stitch the other pocket.

5. Position one pocket right side up over one runner right side, vertically centered on the runner with the pocket lower point 3" from the runner lower point; pin (**E**). Overcast stitch around the pocket side and lower edges. Repeat to stitch the other pocket to the other runner end.

6. Right sides facing, pin the runners together. Stitch around the perimeter, beginning at one long-edge center. Leave a 6" opening for turning (**F**).

7. Turn the runner right side out. Use a knitting needle to push out the seams and corners. Finger-press the runner edges.

8. Fold the runner opening seam allowance open; finger-press. Topstitch around the runner edges using a ⅜" seam allowance.

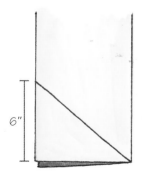

C Draw line connecting mark to lower edge.

6"

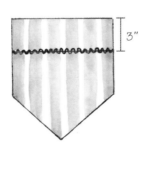

D Stitch raw short edge.

3"

E Position pocket on runner; pin.

3"

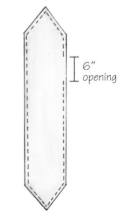

F Stitch around runner, leaving opening for turning.

6" opening

Don't iron Sunbrella fabric unless your iron has a Teflon plate. If it does, use a very low heat setting.

drink umbrellas

BY AMY STALP

TURN A SIMPLE GLASS OF WATER OR LEMONADE into a summertime treat with these bright drink umbrellas. They're perfect for bringing a little extra cheer and color to a summer picnic or an afternoon spent lounging by the pool.

instructions

1. From the solid fabric, cut four 6″ squares. From the interfacing, cut eight 6″ squares.

2. Fuse one interfacing square to each fabric square wrong side.

3. Using the pattern on page 45 and the fabric-marking pen, trace one umbrella on each solid fabric square right side. Transfer all markings from the pattern to the fabric.

4. Spray one solid fabric square wrong side with temporary spray adhesive. Wrong sides facing, position the square over one print fabric square. Repeat to attach each remaining solid square to one print square.

5. Cut out each umbrella. On each umbrella, cut one spoke, cutting up to, but not through, the center (**A**).

6. Set the sewing machine for a 2.5 mm-wide, 0.5 mm-long zigzag stitch. Thread the top and bobbin with matching thread.

7. Working with the solid fabric side up on one umbrella, stitch all but one spoke and the cut spoke. Begin stitching just past the center and stitch outward; trim the threads (**B**).

To make all of the umbrellas from the same print fabric, purchase ¼ yard of fabric instead of four 6″ squares.

YOU WILL NEED:

(makes four umbrellas)

- 6″ square each of four print fabrics
- ¼ yard of solid fabric
- ⅓ yard of fusible interfacing
- temporary spray adhesive
- fabric-marking pen
- matching all-purpose thread
- 4 wooden skewers

A Cut out umbrella; cut one spoke.

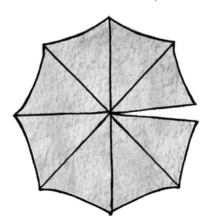

B Stitch spokes.

take cover

THE HOLE TRUTH

When poking a hole through the umbrellas, be very careful not to make the hole too large. If the hole is too big, the umbrella won't stay on the skewer and it might end up in your drink.

8. Overlap the cut spoke with one section; stitch (**C**). Trim the underlap section approximately ¼" past the stitching.

9. Stitch the umbrella outer edge, letting the right needle swing stitch just off the fabric edge (**D**).

10. Fold the umbrella along each spoke; press.

11. Using the point of a sharp scissors, poke a small hole through the umbrella center. Insert a wooden skewer through the hole.

12. Repeat for the remaining three umbrellas.

C Overlap sections; stitch.

D Stitch around umbrella.

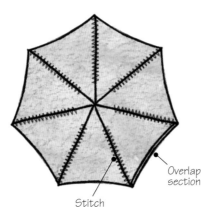

Overlap section

Stitch

Drink Umbrella Pattern

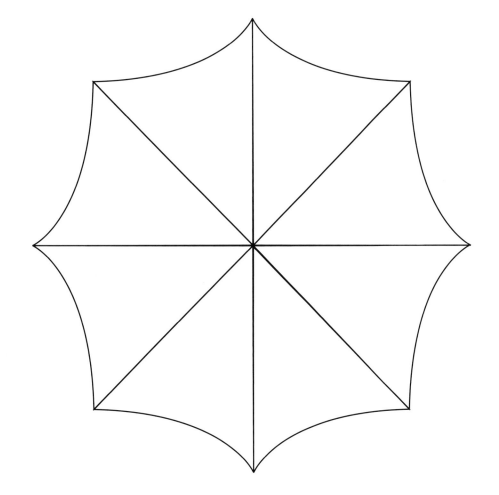

Cut 4.

fleece floor pillow

BY AMY STALP

THIS BIG COMFY PILLOW is the perfect fix for an apartment or dorm room with limited seating options. Stitch up several pillows so you're instantly ready to entertain a crowd.

instructions

Stitch all seams right sides together with a ½" seam allowance unless otherwise indicated. Finger-press open all seams.

1. From the orange fleece, cut one 7"x13" rectangle, two 7"x19" rectangles and two 17"x31" rectangles.

2. From the pink fleece, cut five 7" squares and one 13" square.

3. From the green fleece, cut one 7"x 13" rectangle and two 7"x 19" rectangles.

4. Stitch one 7" pink square to the 7"x 13" orange rectangle. Stitch the 7"x 13" green rectangle to the 13" pink square. Stitch the two rectangles together to form the center square (**A**).

5. Stitch one 7"x 19" orange rectangle to the square upper edge. Stitch one 7"x 19" green rectangle to the square lower edge (**B**).

6. Stitch one 7" pink square to each short end of one 7"x 19" green rectangle. Stitch one 7" pink square to each short end of one 7"x 19" orange rectangle (**C**).

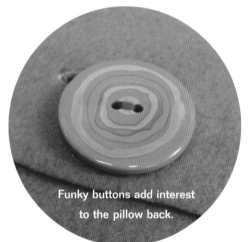

Funky buttons add interest to the pillow back.

A Stitch center square.

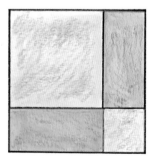

B Stitch upper and lower rectangles.

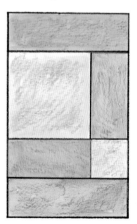

C Stitch pink squares to ends.

7. Stitch the green pieced strip to the square left edge. Stitch the orange pieced strip to the square right edge (**D**).

8. On one 17″x 31″ orange rectangle, measure and mark three evenly spaced buttonholes,

positioning the first one 1″ from one 31″ edge. Stitch a 1⅜″ buttonhole at each mark (**E**). Cut open each buttonhole, being careful not to cut the stitching. Apply seam sealant to prevent raveling.

9. To create the pillow back, overlap the two 17″x31″ orange rectangles to form a 31″ square placing the square with buttonholes on top; baste (**F**).

10. Aligning the raw edges, stitch the pillow front and back together along the perimeter. Clip the corners, and turn the pillow right side out.

11. Mark the button positions under the buttonholes; hand stitch one button at each marked position.

12. Insert the pillow form and button the pillow.

D Stitch side rectangles.

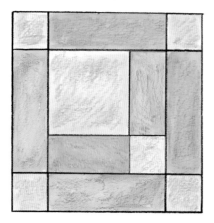

E Stitch buttonholes.

F Baste pillow back.

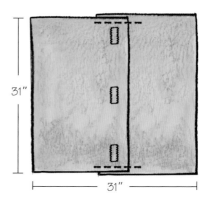

31″

31″

envelope pillow

BY LINDA LEE

THIS CLEVER PILLOW IS GREAT for showcasing a beautiful fabric. Using a chopstick as a closure gives the pillow a unique twist.

Finished size: 12″ x 16″

instructions

pattern

Refer to figure A as a guide for making the pattern.

1. Draw a 16″ x 34″ rectangle on pattern paper. Mark the upper-edge center.

2. Mark a point 4″ down from each upper corner. Draw diagonal lines from the upper-edge center to each point on the sides to create cutting lines for the pillow overlap.

3. Draw a horizontal line 10″ down from the upper-edge center to create a cutting line for the overlap facing.

4. Draw a horizontal line 12″ from the lower edge to use as a foldline for the pillow lower edge.

5. Add ½″ to each edge for seam allowances.

6. Cut one pillow piece from the fabric. Use chalk to transfer the foldline onto the fabric.

7. Cut one overlap facing piece from the same or contrasting fabric, cutting it off at the facing cutline.

construction

Use ½″ seam allowances.

1. Finish the pillow lower edge (**B**). Press the finished edge ½″ toward the wrong side and topstitch in place .

*Finish the raw edges of this pillow using one of the following methods: Use pinking shears, zigzag the edges on the sewing machine or overlock them using a serger.

YOU WILL NEED:

- ½ yard of fabric (non-directional motif) or 1 yard of fabric (directional motif)
- ⅓ yard of fabric for facing (additional fabric needed only if contrasting)
- all-purpose thread
- 1 chopstick
- 2″ of ½″-wide elastic
- 12″ x 16″ pillow form
- pattern paper

● ● ● ● ●

A Make pattern.

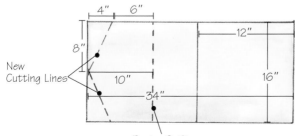

New Cutting Lines

B Finish pillow lower edge.

2. With right sides together, fold the pillow lower edge along the foldline and pin in place at the side seams (**C**).

3. Finish the overlap facing lower edge. With right sides together, position the facing on the pillow, overlapping the facing over the pillow hemmed edge 2″; pin. Stitch the side seams and the overlap edges (**D**). Finish the edges.

4. Turn the pillow right side out. Press the overlap edges so the facing fabric doesn't show.

5. Mark a buttonhole placement 3½″ from the point, centering it on the overlap. Stitch one machine buttonhole horizontally and cut it open (**E**).

6. Insert the pillow form. Position the overlap where you want it. Use pins to poke through the buttonhole, marking the placement of the elastic loop on the pillow.

7. Remove the pillow form. Wrap the elastic around the chopstick to determine how much is required for the loop. Add enough to the loop length to sew to the pillow. Either hand tack or machine stitch the elastic loop ends to the pillow.

8. Insert the pillow form again. Bring the elastic loop through the buttonhole and insert the chopstick through the loop.

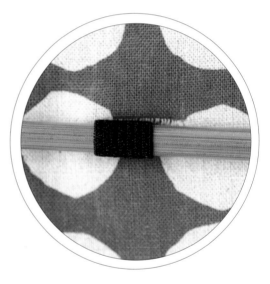

C Fold lower edge; pin.

D Stitch side seams and overlap edges.

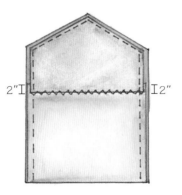

2″I 2″

E Stitch buttonhole.

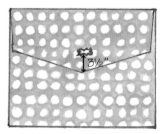

3½″

flange accent pillow

BY LINDA LEE

YOU WILL NEED:

- ½ yard of silk (pillow)

- ½ yard of cotton flannel (underlining)

- ¼ yard of contrasting cotton fabric (flange)

- scrap of contrasting fabric (frame)

- ¼ yard of 3″-wide ribbon

- paper-backed fusible web

- matching all-purpose thread

- 14″ x 18″ pillow form

● ● ● ● ●

BEAUTIFUL PRINTED RIBBON TAKES CENTER STAGE on this elegant pillow. Use rich silk fabric for the pillow and accent it with contrasting flange. The result is a stunning accessory for your home.

instructions

All seams are ½″ unless otherwise indicated.

1. From the silk, cut two 14″ x 18″ rectangles (pillow front and back). From the cotton flannel, cut two 14″ x 18″ rectangles. From the flange fabric, cut two 3″ x 14″ and two 3″ x 18″ strips. From the frame fabric, cut two ½″ x 10″ strips and two ½″x 4″ strips. From the paper-backed fusible web, cut two ½″x 10″ strips, two ½″ x 4″ strips and one 3″ x 9″ rectangle.

2. Fuse the paper-backed fusible web to the wrong side of the frame fabric strips and the ribbon.

3. Remove the paper backing from the ribbon. Center the ribbon on the pillow front; fuse in place.

4. Remove the paper backing from the ½″ x 10″ frame fabric strips, and position them along the upper and lower ribbon edges, overlapping them slightly; fuse in place. Repeat, positioning the ½″ x 4″ frame strips over the left and right ribbon edges. Zizgag stitch along both edges of the frame strips (**A**).

5. Wrong sides together, baste one cotton flannel rectangle to the pillow front. Repeat, basting the remaining cotton flannel rectangle to the pillow back.

6. Fold the short end of each flange fabric strip to the wrong side ½″. Fold each strip in half lengthwise wrong sides together; press (**B**).

7. Matching raw edges, position the folded flange strips on the pillow front right side. Center each strip; the ends will be ½″ from the fabric edges. Baste each strip in place (**C**).

8. Right sides together stitch the pillow front and back, leaving an opening along the lower edge.

9. Turn the pillow right side out. Insert the pillow form, and slipstitch the opening closed.

A Stitch frame.

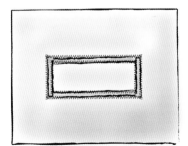

B Fold and press strips.

C Baste flange strips.

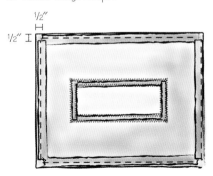

Get to the point

tab-top curtains

BY DONNA BABYLON

YOU'LL BE PLEASANTLY SURPRISED at how easy it is to make these unlined tab curtains. The simplicity of this window treatment style allows luscious fabric be the star of any room in your home.

measuring

Before measuring, install the curtain rod you'll be using. To determine the curtain's finished dimensions, measure the window width from outside edge to outside edge including the trim. Measure the curtain length from the upper edge of the window frame to where you want the lower edge of the curtain to be. **Note:** Floor-length curtains should be ½" off the floor.

Consider the following things when determining the curtain's finished dimensions:

• Do you want the curtain full and gathered or straight with little or no gathering? For a fuller curtain, you should multiply the width by 1½ or 2 to achieve the desired effect.

• Curtains are usually larger than the window they're covering.

• The position of the curtain rod affects the length of the tabs. The top of the curtain should hide the window trim.

After you know the curtain's finished dimensions, you'll need to allow extra fabric for other construction elements. For a tab curtain, add:

• 6" to the width for the side hems

• 8½" to the length for the lower hem and upper edge seam allowance

• ½ yard for the tabs

• Cut a rectangle that measures 3½" by the curtain width for the facing.

DETERMINING TAB LENGTH

To determine the exact length of the tab, drape a fabric strip over the rod and pin it together at the upper edge of the window frame. Pin-mark this position on both sides of the fabric strip before removing it from the rod. Measure the distance between the marks and add 1" to this measurement. Cut the tabs 5" wide by this length.

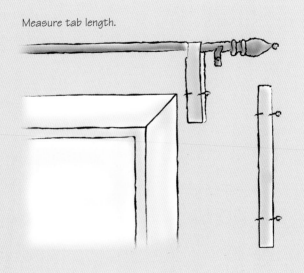

Measure tab length.

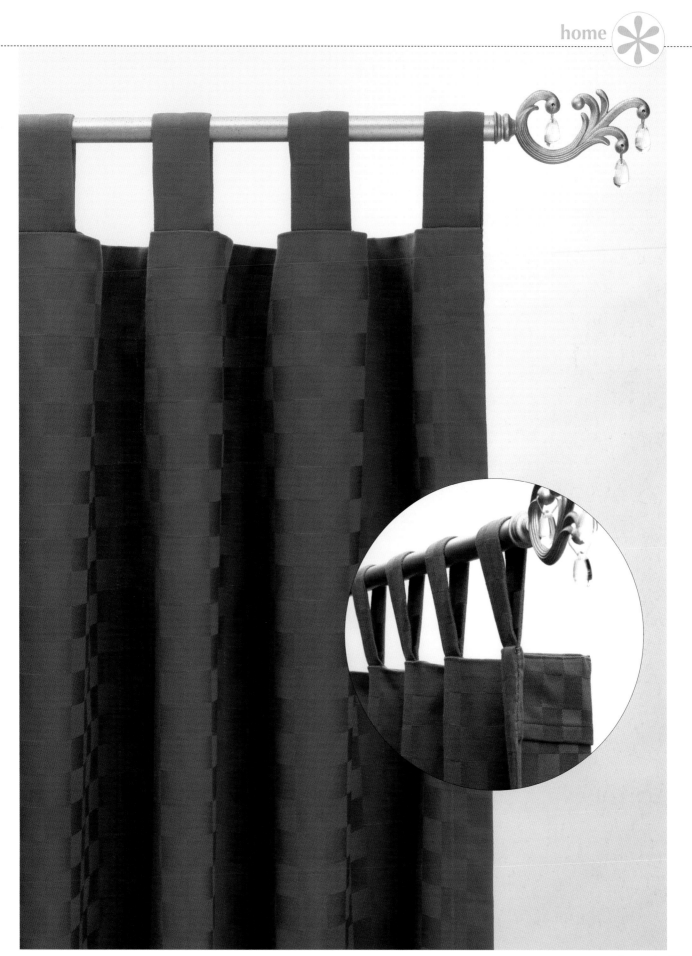

HEMS

For a professional look for any style of window treatment, make the hems as inconspicuous as possible. Do as the professionals do and blindstitch the hems (most home sewing machines have this feature). A blindstitch consists of several straight stitches and one zigzag stitch. Test the stitch on a fabric scrap from your project to adjust the width of the zigzag stitch. You want the resulting stitch to be as invisible as possible on the right side.

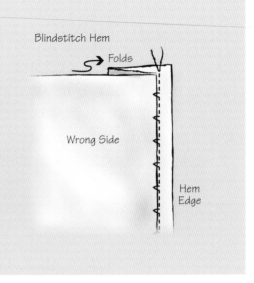

Blindstitch Hem

Folds

Wrong Side

Hem Edge

instructions

1. Cut the fabric according to the determined measurements.

2. To hem the curtain, turn under 8″ along the lower edge; press. Fold under the hem raw edge to meet the pressed crease; press the second fold. Stitch close to the upper folded edge (**A**).

3. To hem the side edges, turn under 3″ along each side edge; press. Fold under the raw edge to meet the pressed crease; press again. Stitch close to the second folded edge of the hem (**B**).

4. Right sides together, fold each tab strip in half lengthwise. Stitch the long edge to form a tube. Press the seam open. Turn each tab right side out and position the seam in the middle of one side; press flat (**C**).

5. Fold each tab in half crosswise with the seam inside the fold and align the ends.

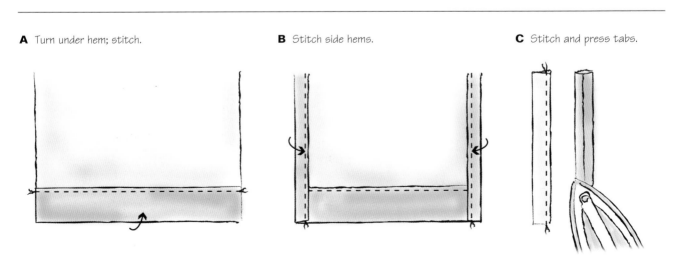

A Turn under hem; stitch.

B Stitch side hems.

C Stitch and press tabs.

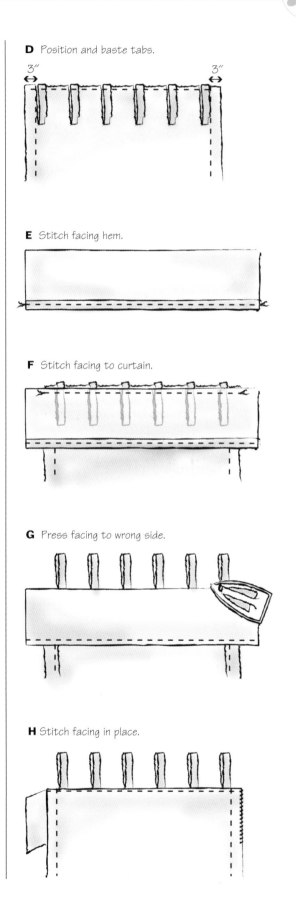

D Position and baste tabs.

3″   3″

E Stitch facing hem.

F Stitch facing to curtain.

G Press facing to wrong side.

H Stitch facing in place.

6. Determine the placement of the tabs along the curtain upper edge. Position the outer edges of the first and last tab 3″ from each side edge; evenly space the remaining tabs between the end tabs, approximately 5″-6″ apart. **Note:** The more space between the tabs, the more this area will drape down when hung on the rod.

7. Position the tabs on the curtain upper edge, aligning the raw edges; baste (**D**).

8. To prepare the facing, fold under one long edge ½″; press. Fold under ½″ again and press, making a double ½″ hem. Stitch (**E**).

9. Right sides together, stitch the facing raw edge to the curtain upper edge, sandwiching the tabs between the curtain and the facing. The facing will extend beyond the curtain's hemmed sides (**F**).

10. Fold the facing over to the curtain wrong side; press (**G**). **Optional:** Stitch close to the upper edge through all layers to prevent the facing from showing on the right side.

11. Turn under the facing raw edges on each side, tucking them between the curtain and the facing for a smooth finish. Hand stitch in place to secure (**H**).

SOURCE | **Hancock Fabrics,** (877) 322-7427, hancockfabrics.com, donated the fabric.

embellished tabs

BY DONNA BABYLON

TABS DON'T HAVE TO BE JUST PLAIN blocks of fabric that hold curtains in place. Consider them an opportunity to be creative and play. Take tabs from functional to fabulous with these easy-sew embellishment techniques.

All seams are ½″ unless otherwise indicated.

measuring

To determine the tab finished length (the part of the tab that's visible minus any seam allowances), drape a fabric strip over the curtain rod and pin it together at the upper edge of the window frame. Pin-mark this position on both sides of the fabric strip before removing it from the rod. Measure the distance between the pins—this is the finished length (**A**). For a standard cut length measurement, add 1″ for seam allowances.

decorative stitch tab

Put your machine's built-in decorative stitches to good use and create a one-of-a-kind tab. Use one stitch or make your own design by combining two or more stitches. To create the featured stitch, combine short rows of satin stitching.

1. Make a sample of the stitch on scrap fabric. Measure the width of the stitch and add 3″. This is the cut width of the tab.

2. Add 1″ to the finished length of the tab for the cut length. (See "Measuring" at left to determine the tab finished length.)

3. Cut tabs to these measurements.

4. Stitch down the center of each tab (**B**).

5. Refer to "Finishing the Tabs" on page 62 to attach the tabs to the curtain.

ribbon tab

An embroidered ribbon adds excitement to a plain tab. Select one that incorporates the colors in the room.

1. Measure the width of the ribbon and add 4″. This is the cut width of the tab.

A Measure tab length.

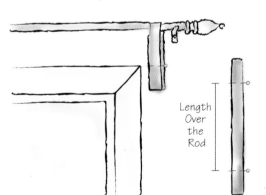

Length Over the Rod

B Stitch down center of tab.

Decorative
Stitch Tab

Ribbon Tab

Two-Tone
Twisted Tab

2. Add 1″ to the finished length of the tab for the cut length. (See "Measuring" on page 58 to determine the tab finished length.)

3. Cut tabs to these measurements.

4. Center the ribbon on the tab. Edgestitch both ribbon long edges (**C**).

5. Refer to "Finishing the Tabs" on page 62 to attach the tabs to the curtain.

two-tone twisted tab

This easy-to-make tab style is a clever way to introduce an accent color to your décor.

1. For each tab, cut 3″x14″ strips from two different fabrics (you'll trim the length later to the correct measurement).

2. Right sides together, stitch the strips along each lengthwise edge (**D**). Turn the tab right side out, and press it flat so neither fabric is visible from the opposite side.

3. Fold the strip in half widthwise to find the center. Twist the tab one complete turn so the same color fabric is touching (**E**).

4. Align the cut edges; pin. Trim the ends ½″ beyond the finished tab length measurement. Baste the edges.

5. Refer to "Inserting Tabs and Finishing the Top Edge" on page 62 to attach the tabs to the curtain.

corded tab

Cording adds a touch of color and a classy finish to an otherwise plain tab. Choose matching cording for a subtle effect or contrasting cording to make a bolder statement.

1. For each tab, cut two 3″-wide strips by the cut length measurement. Cut two lengths of cording to the cut length measurement.

2. Insert a zipper or cording foot in the sewing machine.

3. Position the cording on the fabric strip right side as shown. Begin and end the seam by bending the cord so it's flush with the end seam allowance; untwist the cord in the seam allowance to flatten the cords.

C Edgestitch ribbon long edges.

D Stitch lengthwise edges.

E Twist tab.

4. Baste the cording in place, stitching as close to the cord as possible. Stitch over the flattened cord section. Repeat on the opposite edge (**F**).

5. Right sides together, meet the corded strip and the remaining strip. Stitch directly on the basting stitches.

6. Turn the tab right side out.

7. Refer to "Inserting Tabs and Finishing the Top Edge" on page 62 to attach the tabs to the curtain.

button tab

Extend the tab over the front edge to create this look. Add a button to secure the tab in place. **Note:** For a perfect match, use 1⅛" covered button forms with the curtain fabric. Or purchase contrasting buttons to make them stand out.

1. For each tab, cut 5"-wide fabric strips by the tab finished length plus 2½" for overlap and seam allowances.

2. Right sides facing, fold each tab strip in half lengthwise. Stitch the long edge to form a tube. Press the seam open; center the seam.

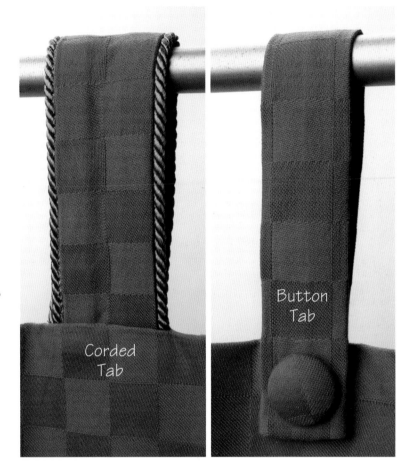

Corded Tab

Button Tab

3. Stitch across one short end of the strip (**G**). Turn the tab right side out; press flat.

4. Place the tab along the curtain upper edge with the tab seam facing the curtain fabric right side. Refer to "Inserting Tabs and Finishing the Top Edge" on page 62.

F Baste cording in place.

G Stitch across one short end

FINISHING THE TABS

1. Fold each tab in half lengthwise. Stitch the long edge to form a tube. Press the seam open. Turn the tab right side out; center the seam. Press the tab flat.

2. Fold each tab in half crosswise with the seam inside the fold; align the cut edges.

3. Go to "Inserting Tabs and Finishing the Top Edge" below.

inserting tabs & finishing the top edge

1. Determine the tab placement along the curtain upper edge. Position the outer edges of the first and last tab 3″ from each side edge; evenly space the remaining tabs between the end tabs. **Note:** The more space between the tabs, the more this area will drape down when hung on the rod.

2. Pin the tabs to the curtain upper edge, aligning the raw edges; baste (**H**).

3. To prepare the facing, fold under one long edge ½″; press. Fold under ½″ again and press, making a double ½″ hem; stitch (**I**).

4. Right sides together, stitch the facing raw edge to the curtain upper edge, sandwiching the tabs between the curtain and the facing. The facing will extend beyond the curtain's hemmed sides (**J**).

5. Fold the facing to the curtain wrong side; press (**K**). Optional: Stitch close to the upper edge through all layers to prevent the facing from showing on the right side.

6. Turn under the facing raw edges on each side, tucking them between the curtain and the facing for a smooth finish. Hand stitch in place to secure (**L**).

H Position and baste tabs.

I Stitch facing hem.

J Stitch facing to curtain.

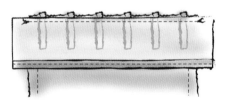

K Press facing to wrong side.

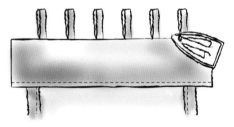

L Stitch facing in place.

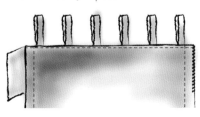

SOURCE | **Hancock Fabrics**, (877) 322-7427, hancockfabrics.com, provided the brown fabric.

curtains

BY AMY STALP

YOU WILL NEED:

• fabric (see "Measuring" to determine yardage.)

● ● ● ● ●

WHEN YOU KNOW HOW TO SEW, you can change the color scheme of a room in an afternoon by stitching up some new curtains. Add some pillows to accent the look. Redecorating will be so easy—you just might become addicted.

measuring

Before measuring, install the curtain rod you'll be using. To determine the finished dimensions of the curtain, measure the window width from outside edge to outside edge. Measure the length from the curtain rod to where you want the curtain lower edge to be (**A**).

Consider the following things when determining the curtain's finished dimensions:

• Do you want the curtain full and gathered or straight with little or no gathering? For a very full curtain, you may wish to double or triple the width to achieve the desired effect.

• Curtains are usually larger than the window they're covering.

• The position of the curtain rod affects the length.

• Adding a header above the rod casing affects the length.

After you know the curtain's finished dimensions, you'll need to allow extra fabric for seam allowances, hems and casing. For a basic curtain, add:

• 2″ to the width for the side hems.

• 2½″ to the length for the lower hem.

• 3″ to the length for the upper casing or hem. (See "Measuring the Rod" on page 64 to make sure you've added enough fabric for the casing to fit over your curtain rod.)

A Measure window for desired result.

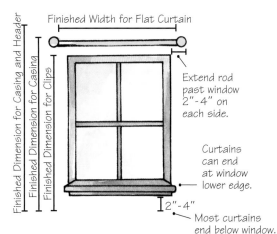

Finished Width for Flat Curtain

Finished Dimension for Casing and Header
Finished Dimension for Casing
Finished Dimension for Clips

Extend rod past window 2″–4″ on each side.

Curtains can end at window lower edge.

2″–4″ — Most curtains end below window.

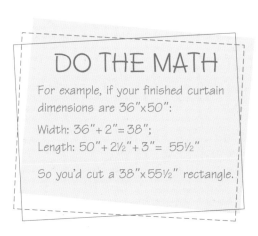

DO THE MATH

For example, if your finished curtain dimensions are 36″x50″:

Width: 36″+ 2″=38″;
Length: 50″+ 2½″+ 3″= 55½″

So you'd cut a 38″x 55½″ rectangle.

MEASURING THE ROD

For a curtain that hangs from a rod, the casing needs to be wide enough to slip over it. Take a few minutes to measure to make sure the curtain will slide easily over the rod.

- Measure around the widest part of the rod you'll use to hang the curtain.
- Add 1″ to the measurement, and divide that number by 2.
- The resulting number is the distance you should allow between stitching lines.

instructions

1. Cut the fabric according to the determined measurements.

2. Hem the side edges. Turn under one side edge ½″; press. Turn under ½″ again; press. Stitch close to the inner fold. Repeat on the opposite side (**B**).

3. To hem the lower edge, turn under ½″ along the lower edge; press. Turn under another 2″ along the lower edge; press. Stitch close to the upper folded edge of the hem.

4. Finish the upper edge using one of the variations detailed below.

hemmed edge—hang with clips

1. Hem the upper edge by turning under 1½″; press. Turn under 1½″ again; press.

2. Stitch close to the lower fold.

3. Attach the curtain clips to the curtain upper edge and hang the curtain from the rod.

casing for curtain rod

1. Turn under ½″ along the upper edge; press. Turn under 2½″ along the upper edge; press.

2. Stitch 1″ from the upper folded edge to form a header. Stitch close to the lower folded edge, approximately 1¼″ below the first stitching (**C**). (See "Measuring the Rod," above, and adjust the spacing between the stitching lines to accommodate the rod, if necessary.)

3. Insert the rod into the casing and hang.

B Hem side edges.

C Stitch casing.

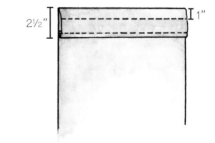

2½″   1″

funky pillowcases

BY AMY STALP

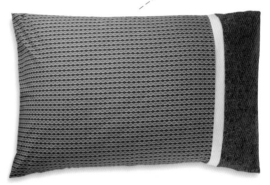

FUN AND FUNKY PILLOWCASES brighten your bedroom and make great traveling companions. Experiment with novelty and seasonal prints. For a quick gift, customize a case using the recipient's favorite colors.

instructions

All seams are ½″ unless otherwise noted.

1. Preshrink the fabrics.

2. Cut one 27″x 42″ rectangle from the main-body fabric. Cut one 11″x 42″ rectangle from the band fabric. To add a narrow trim strip, cut one 3½″x 42″ strip from the trim fabric.

3. With wrong sides together, press the band rectangle in half lengthwise, creating a 5½″x 42″ band. If adding trim, repeat to create a 1¾″x 42″ strip.

4. Matching the long raw edges, baste the folded trim strip to the fabric band (**A**).

5. Pin the band to the right side of the pillowcase along the 42″ edge with raw edges aligned and the trim sandwiched in between; stitch. Zigzag- or serge-finish the seam allowance raw edges and press them toward the pillowcase body.

6. Fold the pillowcase right sides together, matching the band seamline and upper edges, and stitch the raw edges together (**B**).

7. Trim the corners to reduce bulk. Zigzag- or serge-finish the seam allowance raw edges, and turn the pillowcase right side out; press.

YOU WILL NEED:

(makes one standard-size case. For best results, use 100% cotton or cotton/polyester blend fabrics.)

• ⅞ yard of 45″-wide main-body fabric

• ⅓ yard of 45″-wide contrasting-band fabric

• ⅛ yard of 45″-wide trim fabric (optional)

• matching all-purpose thread

A Baste trim to pillowcase band.

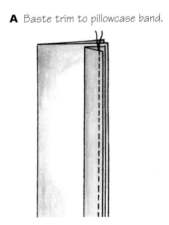

B Stitch pillowcase seams.

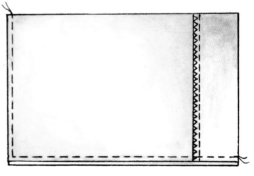

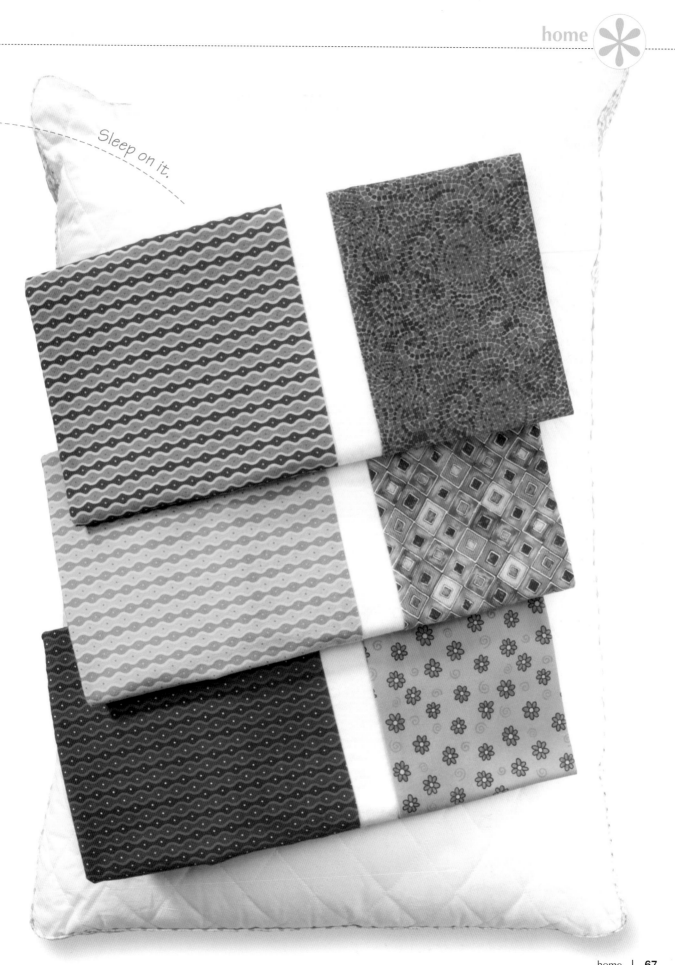

Sleep on it.

patchwork quilt

BY KATE BASHYNSKI

THIS QUILT IS JUST RIGHT FOR COOL SUMMER EVENINGS IN THE HAMMOCK OR GREETING THE SUNRISE OUT ON THE DECK. Fabric squares in your choice of colors and prints give this simple pattern visual appeal. The long rectangular shape makes it a perfect lap quilt for two.

Finished size: 56″ x 91″

instructions

Stitch all seams right sides together with ¼″ seam allowances unless otherwise noted.

1. Cut each yard of fabric into five 6½″-wide strips. Cut each strip into six 6½″ squares.

2. Lay out the squares in 15 rows, alternating rows of nine and ten squares. Emphasize an offset diagonal pattern when arranging the squares (**A**).

3. Aligning the cut edges, stitch all of the squares from each row together. Press the seams flat to set the stitches, and then press open each seam.

4. On the long rows, mark the center of each square along the raw edges (**B**).

5. Lay out the rows, matching the center marks on the long rows to the short row seams (**C**). Right sides facing, pin the rows together at each mark; stitch. Press the seams flat, and then press all the seam allowances in the same direction.

YOU WILL NEED:

- 1 yard each of 5 coordinating fabrics
- lightweight batting at least 4″ larger than the completed quilt top (approximately 58″ x 94″)
- cotton backing at least 6″ larger than the completed quilt top (approximately 60″ x 96″)
- thread: matching all-purpose, quilting
- hand-sewing needle
- erasable fabric-marking pen or pencil

DESIGN IDEAS

- Purchase more than five fabrics or larger yardages to create a larger quilt.
- Cut larger squares; the assembly will be faster and you can cut fewer squares.
- Cut smaller squares to create smaller projects, such as pillows, table runners, and place mats.

A Arrange squares in rows.

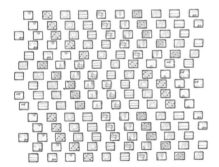

B Mark center of each square.

C Match center marks to seams.

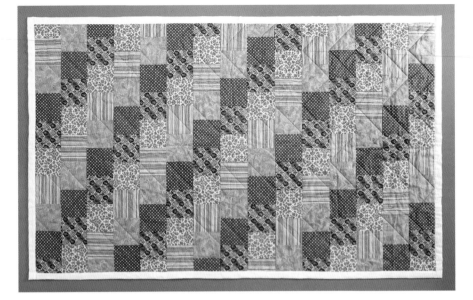

To create a more traditional sized lap quilt, add more squares to each row and reduce the number of rows.

6. When all the rows have been sewn together and pressed, trim the long rows even with the short rows (**D**).

7. Place the backing wrong side up on a hard, smooth surface. Tape the backing edges to the surface, keeping the fabric smooth and wrinkle-free, but not stretched out of shape (**E**).

8. Center the batting over the backing, smoothing it in place.

9. Right side up, center the quilt top over the batting and backing.

10. Thread a hand-sewing needle. Use long running stitches to baste the layers together,

beginning in the middle of the quilt and stitching toward the outer edges. Or pin-baste the layers together using safety pins spaced 5″ to 6″ apart (**F**).

11. Mark the quilt top with stitching lines using an erasable fabric-marking pen or pencil and a ruler. Following the illustration, mark rows of large zigzags (**G**). Remove the tape from the backing edges.

12. Quilt the layers together by hand or machine. See "Making a Quilt" on page 203 for instructions.

13. Remove the pins or thread basting after the quilting is completed.

D Trim along rows even with short rows.

E Tape backing in place.

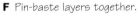

F Pin-baste layers together.

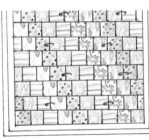

G Mark quilt top.

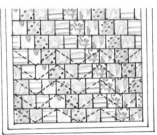

HAND IT OFF

If you enjoyed putting the quilt top together but are uneasy about the quilting, don't be afraid to send your quilt top, batting and backing to a professional quilter. (It's not cheating; many quilters do this.) A local quilt shop will be able to help you locate a quilter. Ask to see samples and get references.

14. Baste around the quilt top, stitching a scant ¼" from the quilt top raw edges through all layers.

15. Trim the batting to extend 1¼" beyond the quilt top.

16. Trim the backing to extend 2" beyond the batting (or a total of 3¼" from the quilt top edge) (**H**).

17. Fold up the backing lengthwise edges ½" toward the quilt top; press (**I**).

18. Bring the backing lengthwise edges over the quilt top edge so the folded edges just cover the basting stitches. Pin along the folded edges.

Machine or hand stitch along the folds, beginning and ending stitching at the batting edges (**J**).

19. Repeat to fold and stitch the backing short edges to the quilt top. Hand stitch the ends to encase all raw edges (**K**).

SOURCES | **Bolines LLC,** (888) 214-3819, bolines.com, carries the fabric used in this project. | **Nancy's Notions,** (800) 833-0690, nancysnotions. com, carries the batting, backing fabric and threads used in this project. | **Pleasant Valley Farm Longarm Quilting,** Manchester, WI, petruske@centurytel.net, provided the machine quilting for this project.

RESOURCES | *Denyse Schmidt Quilts* by Denyse Schmidt; Chronicle Books, 2005. | *Sew Simple Volume 3,* page 20. "Machine Quilting." | *Quilt with Confidence* by Nancy Zieman; Krause Publications, 2007.

H Trim batting and backing.

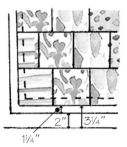

I Fold up backing lengthwise edges.

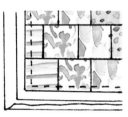

J Stitch along fold.

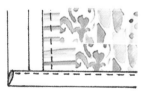

K Hand stitch ends.

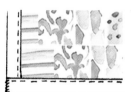

reusable grocery bag

BY BETH BRADLEY

DO YOUR PART TO HELP THE PLANET AND JUST SAY "NO" TO PLASTIC SHOPPING BAGS. Use recycled nylon fabric to sew an eco-friendly alternative. The sturdy, water-resistant and lightweight tote folds up to fit in your purse or pocket for trips to the farmer's market or grocery store.

instructions

Use ½" seam allowances unless otherwise noted.

1. Cut out the tote and facing pieces from the fabric using the pattern on page 75. For the gusset, cut one 4" x 41¾" strip (depending on the size of garment or item you've salvaged, you may need to piece the gusset strip to achieve the required length).

2. Serge- or zigzag-finish one facing lower edge (**A**).

3. Position one pair of tote pieces with right sides facing; pin along the center front edge. Stitch a flat-fell seam (see "Flat-Fell Seam" on page 74) at the tote center front.

4. With right sides facing, position one tote facing over the constructed tote side, aligning the upper edges; pin. Stitch the upper and side edges (**B**). Press the seam allowances toward the facing. Clip the seam allowances around the curves.

5. Turn the tote right side out. Use a knitting needle to push out the edges; press.

YOU WILL NEED:

- salvaged nylon fabric (look for nylon windbreakers, tents or gym bags)
- matching all-purpose or polyester thread

THRIFTY TIPS

When searching the thrift store for fabric to repurpose, keep these tips in mind.

- Make note of the instructions on the original garment care label.
- Garments or items that have large uninterrupted areas of fabric work best for recycling into new projects.
- Use a seam ripper to deconstruct the garment and see how much fabric you have. You may have to get creative with piecing the fabric in order to cut out larger pattern pieces.

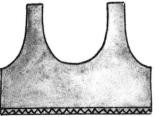
A Serge facing lower edge.

B Stitch upper and side edges.

FLAT-FELL SEAM

Flat-fell seams are used frequently in denim or athletic garment construction because they're extra tough and durable. A flat-fell seam on a grocery tote provides strength to hold all the goodies you gather.

1. Sew a ½" seam with the fabric wrong sides facing. Press open the seam.

2. Trim one seam allowance to ¼" (**1**). Press the trimmed seam allowance toward the wider seam allowance.

3. Fold the wider seam allowance in half, encasing the narrower seam allowance (**2**). Press the fold flat against the fabric; pin.

4. Stitch close to the folded edge (**3**); press.

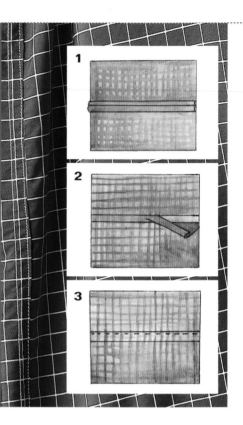

6. Fold each upper handle edge ½" toward the facing side. Overlap the two folded edges; pin. Stitch across the handle close to each folded edge (**C**).

7. Repeat steps 2 through 6 to construct the other tote side and facing.

8. Fold each gusset short edge ⅜" toward the fabric wrong side. Fold again ½" toward the wrong side. Stitch close to the first fold.

9. With right sides facing, pin the gusset along one tote side and lower edges. Stitch the side and lower edges (**D**). For more control, use the hand wheel rather than the presser foot to stitch the lower corners. Press open the side and lower seams. Repeat to attach the other tote side to the gusset.

10. Serge- or zigzag-finish the side and lower tote seams. Turn the tote right side out.

C Stitch handle close to each fold.

D Stitch gusset to tote piece.

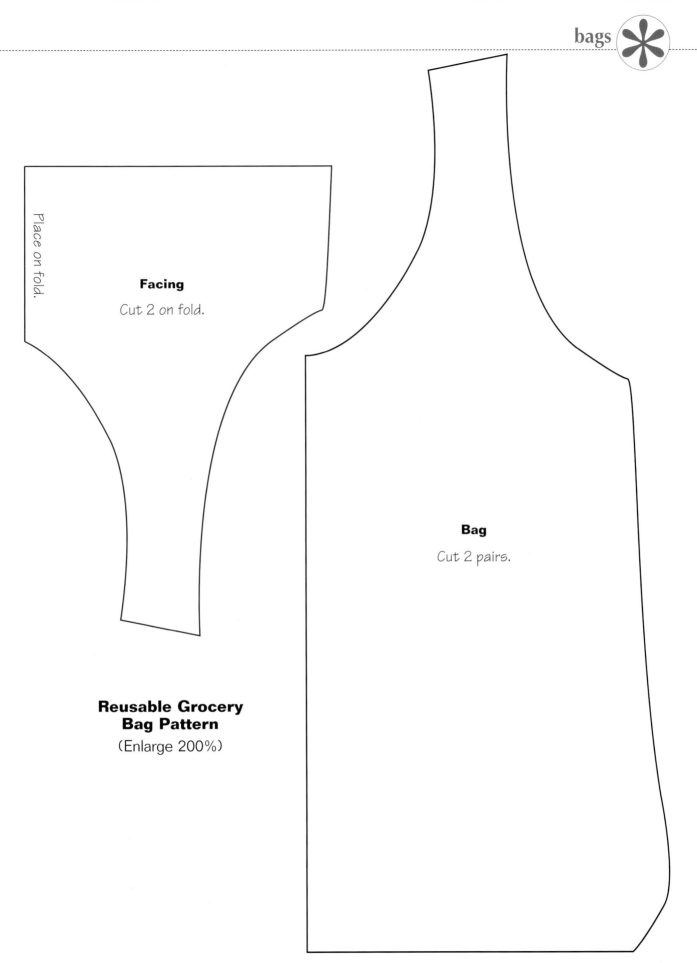

Place on fold.

Facing

Cut 2 on fold.

**Reusable Grocery
Bag Pattern**

(Enlarge 200%)

Bag

Cut 2 pairs.

reversible purse

BY ELLEN MARCH

HAVE TWICE THE FUN WITH TWO PURSES IN ONE. Turn the purse inside out and vice versa to change the look quickly and easily.

instructions

Use ½" seam allowances.

1. Enlarge the pattern on page 78 by 400%. Using the pattern, cut two purses from each fabric.

2. Place one pair of purse pieces on a flat work surface with right sides facing and edges and corners aligned. Stitch the purse pieces together along the upper edge; press open the seam. Stitch the side edges independently; press open. Repeat to stitch the second pair of purse sections together.

3. Stitch the lower edges independently, leaving a 5" opening along one lower-edge center for turning (**A**). Press open the seams.

4. With right sides facing, place one purse section inside the other, aligning all edges. Pin around the outer edge (**B**); stitch, and then press open the seam.

5. Turn the purse right side out through the opening; press.

6. Push one purse section inside the other with wrong sides facing so the opening along one lower edge is exposed. Topstitch the outer edge (**C**).

7. Slipstitch the opening closed. Fold the purse along the upper-edge seam and insert the hand-stitched edge into the opposite lower edge (**D**).

8. Hand stitch each diagonal edge for 5", beginning at the outer-edge corner (**E**). Catch only the outer fabric in the stitching so it doesn't show through on the reverse side. Stitch a button at the corner. Turn the purse inside out, and repeat to stitch the diagonal edges and corner button.

YOU WILL NEED:

- 1 yard each of two coordinating print fabrics
- 2 decorative buttons
- matching all-purpose thread
- hand-sewing needle

SOURCES | **Fabric.com** provided the Amy Butler Belle fabric.

A Stitch side then lower edges; leave opening along one end.

B Pin outer edge.

C Topstitch outer edge.

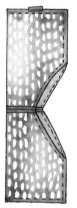

D Insert one purse section into the other.

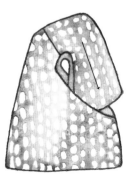

F Hand stitch diagonal edge.

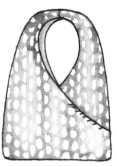

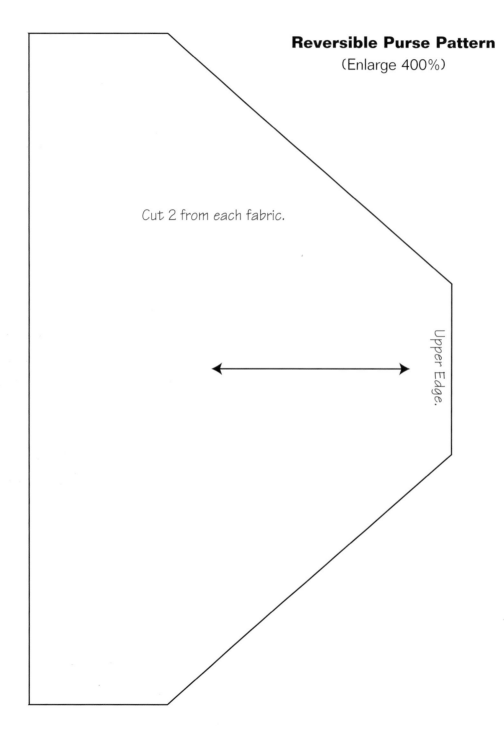

Reversible Purse Pattern

(Enlarge 400%)

Cut 2 from each fabric.

Upper Edge.

messenger bag

BY ELLEN MARCH

THIS TRENDY BAG is quick to make and easy on the budget. Just cut strips of different fabrics and arrange them however you like. Piece the short strips together to make the bag, and the long strips together for the shoulder strap. Add two squares for the lining.

If you're low on cash, consider recycling old blue jeans or corduroys. Traditionally, piecing fabric together was about recycling, but with these fabrics your bag will be strictly contemporary.

instructions

1. From the yardage or pants, cut twelve 3″x 13″ strips for the bag. Cut four 3″x 25″ strips for the strap. Cut two 1½″ x 13″ strips for the tie closure. From the lining fabric, cut two 13″ squares.

2. Insert a jeans needle into the sewing machine. Sew with ½″ seam allowances unless otherwise noted.

3. Lay out six fabric strips for the bag front, arranging the shades and colors to your liking. With right sides together, pin the strip long edges

together and stitch. Repeat for the bag back.

4. Right sides together, pin the bag front to the back and stitch the sides and lower edge. Trim off the corners, turn right side out and press.

5. Right sides facing, stitch two strap pieces together at one short end. Repeat for the remaining two strap pieces.

6. Pin the two resulting strips right sides together and stitch both long edges. Machine baste one short end closed for aid in turning. Press the seams open to make pressing and stitching easier in the next step.

7. Turn the strap right side out. Use a yardstick or dowel to gently push the strap closed end back through the tube (**A**). Remove the basting and press the strap flat with the seams at each edge. Edgestitch both long edges.

8. With right sides together and raw edges even, stitch the strap ends to the bag upper edges, centering the strap ends over the side seams, and making sure the strap isn't twisted (**B**).

YOU WILL NEED:

- ¼ yard each of three or more pieces of 60″-wide fabric, or two or more pairs of colored cords or jeans faded to different shades

- ⅜ yard of lining fabric

- matching all-purpose thread

- jeans sewing-machine needle

A Turn strap right side out.

B Stitch strap to bag.

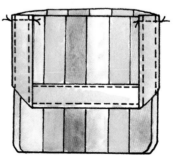

OR MAKE A TOTE

If you prefer a shorter strap, turn your messenger bag into a tote to be worn over your shoulder. Simply shorten the strap to approximately 28" long.

Cut two 3"x30" strips for the strap. Construct the strap as described in steps 6 and 7 and complete the bag.

9. For the tie closure, press under ¼" on one short edge of the two 1½"x13" strips. Press the strips in half lengthwise. Open each strip and press the two long raw edges toward the center fold, press. Press again on the first fold to create a double-fold tie. Edgestitch the ties to secure the folds (**C**).

10. Center one tie on the front and one on the back on the purse upper edge and baste in place (**D**).

11. Pin the two lining squares right sides together. Leaving one side open for the upper edge, stitch the lining pieces together along the side and lower edges, leaving a 4" opening along the lower edge. You'll use the opening to turn everything right side out to complete the bag.

12. Slide the pieced bag inside the lining so right sides are together and the upper raw edges are even; pin. Make sure to tuck the straps and ties down inside the bag so they're out of the way. Stitch the bag to the lining around the upper edge, catching the strap ends and ties in the stitching. Turn the bag right side out through the opening in the lining. Press the bag upper edge.

13. Pull the lining back out of the bag, turn in the opening raw edges, and edgestitch or slipstitch closed. Tuck the lining down inside the bag.

SOURCE | **The Carol Harris Co.**, (877) 269-9419, carolharrisco.com, provided the corduroy.

C Fold and stitch ties.

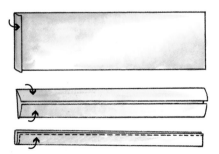

D Baste ties to bag.

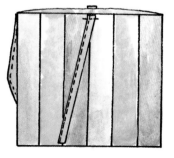

zipper tote

BY LINDA LEE

THIS STYLISH ZIPPER TOTE holds all of your essentials securely. Choose a sturdy fabric in a striking graphic print to make a bold statement.

YOU WILL NEED:

(Finished size: 9½" x 12½" x 4½")

- ½ yard of heavyweight fabric, such as cotton canvas (fabric A)

- ⅛ yard of mediumweight contrast fabric (fabric B)

- two 18½"-long pieces of 1½"-wide webbing

- one 12" decorative metal zipper

- matching all-purpose thread

- sewing machine zipper foot

● ● ● ● ●

instructions

Use ½" seam allowances.

1. From fabric A, cut two 15" x 16¾" rectangles. Cut a 2¼" square from the two lower corners of each rectangle (**A**). From fabric B, cut two 3" x 8½" strips.

2. Serge- or zigzag-finish one fabric A rectangle side and lower edges. Mark the center point along the rectangle upper edge. Mark 1½" to the left and right of the center mark. Pin the ends of one webbing strap to the fabric rectangle right side upper edge, aligning the strap inner edges with the outer marks. Baste across the strap ends (**B**).

3. To create the zipper flange, fold one 3" x 8½" strip in half lengthwise with right sides facing;

press. Stitch across each strip end (**C**). Turn the strip right side out; press.

4. Center the flange over the fabric A rectangle, aligning the flange lengthwise raw edge with the rectangle upper edge and sandwiching the strap; pin. Baste along the flange raw edge through all the layers (**D**). Repeat steps 1 through 4 to create the other bag piece.

Tie the look together with a multicolor zipper.

Add a lining to the bag by fusing light- to mediumweight fabric to the fabric A rectangles before beginning construction.

A Cut squares from lower corners.

B Baste across strap ends.

C Stitch across strip end

D Baste along flange raw edge.

6. Right sides facing, insert the main body inside the lining body. Align the seams and upper edges; pin, making sure the straps are tucked inside and away from the stitching line. Stitch along the upper edge.

7. Turn the tote right side out through the lining opening. Slipstitch the opening closed. Push the lining inside the main body and press the upper edge. Edgestitch along the upper edge.

8. Fold the upper edge 1″ toward the wrong side; press. Be careful to avoid pressing over the nylon webbing straps. Unfold the upper edge. Pin-mark the center point along one side of the upper edge ½″ below the foldline (**B**).

9. Stitch a ½″-wide horizontal buttonhole at the pin mark. Apply seam sealant to the buttonhole if desired; cut open the buttonhole.

10. Refold the tote upper edge along the foldline. Stitch, following the previous stitching line to create a casing. Stitch across the straps along the tote upper edge (**C**).

11. Pin a safety pin to one ribbon end. Insert the safety pin in the buttonhole and feed the ribbon through the casing. Use the safety pin to ease the ribbon through the casing and back out through the buttonhole. Tie a knot in each ribbon end, and then tie the ribbon into a bow.

SOURCE | **Seattle Fabrics,** seattlefabrics.com, supplied the nylon webbing.

✳ Find sailboat- or seashell-print fabric and use rope as the drawstring for a nautical inspired bag.

B Pin-mark buttonhole placement.

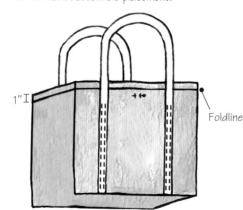

1″

Foldline

C Stitch over straps at tote upper edge.

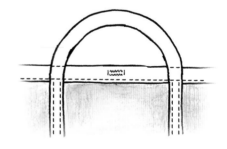

aloha

big summer bag

BY LINDA PERMANN

MAKE THIS ROOMY TOTE TO HOLD ALL OF YOUR BEACH NECESSITIES. Finish it in just a few hours and then head to the shore in style!

instructions

Use ½" seam allowances unless otherwise noted.

1. Trace the pattern on page 91 onto pattern paper; cut it out. Cut two bag pieces each from the canvas, lining fabric and interfacing. Trim the interfacing pieces by ½" around the outer edges.

2. Center one interfacing piece over one canvas-piece wrong side. Fuse according to the manufacturer's instructions. Repeat for the other canvas piece.

3. Right sides facing, pin the canvas pieces together. Stitch around the side and lower edges (**A**). Repeat for the lining-fabric pieces.

4. Clip the lining lower curves. Turn the lining right side out; press.

5. Right sides facing, position the lining inside the bag. Align the bag and lining upper edges; pin. Stitch around the upper edge, beginning before one handle tab and ending after the second handle tab (**B**).

6. Turn the bag right side out through the opening; press. Press the opening edges ½" toward the wrong side; pin.

7. With contrasting thread, stitch around the bag upper edge, making sure to catch the folded opening edges.

8. Insert one handle tab through one handle, folding the tab 1½" toward the lining side; pin. Hand sew the handle-tab edge to the lining fabric, making sure not to catch the canvas fabric in the stitching (**C**). Repeat for the second handle.

YOU WILL NEED:

- 1¼ yards of heavyweight canvas fabric

- 1¼ yards of light- to mediumweight cotton fabric (lining)

- 1¼ yards of mediumweight fusible interfacing

- one pair of 8"-wide bamboo handles

- matching and contrasting all-purpose thread

- pattern paper

- hand-sewing needle

- one 1"-diameter button (optional)

- embroidery floss (optional)

- safety pin (optional)

● ● ● ● ●

A Stitch side and lower edges.

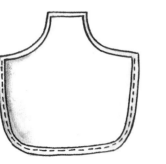

B Stitch around upper edge.

C Hand stitch handle tab.

BRAND NEW BAG

It's easy to personalize the bag by adding extra details and embellishments.

- Add an appliqué design to the bag exterior before sewing the bag together.
- If you're using floral-print fabric, stitch buttons at the flower centers. Or sew buttons randomly across the fabric.
- Attach ribbon or beaded trim to the bag exterior upper edges before sewing the bag together.
- Replace the interfacing layer with quilt batting. After topstitching the bag upper edge, quilt the whole bag for added texture.

9. Turn the bag inside out. Hand stitch the lining corners to the canvas-corners seam allowance (**D**).

10. For the optional flower pin, cut a 3″ x 45″ strip from the lining fabric. Freehand cut large scallops along one strip edge. Baste the strip straight edge, leaving long thread tails.

11. Pull the thread tails tightly to gather the fabric. Coil the gathered strip into a flower shape. With embroidery floss, hand stitch the fabric layers together at the flower center (**E**). Stitch the button at the flower center. Attach the flower to the bag with the safety pin.

RESOURCE | **Reprodepot.com** provided the canvas and cotton fabric and the bamboo handles.

D Hand stitch lining corners.

E Stitch fabric layers together.

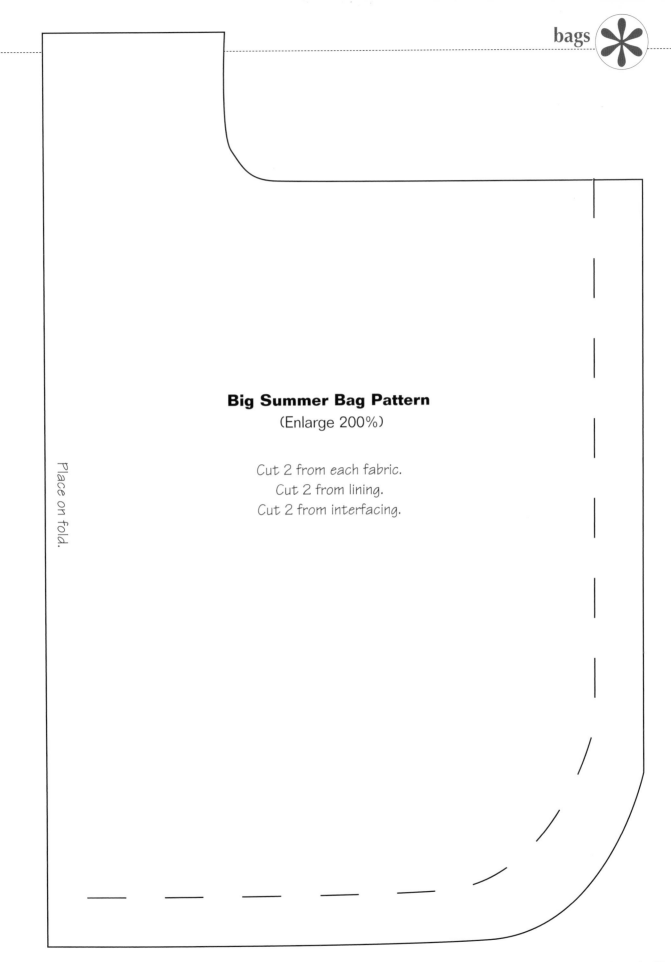

Big Summer Bag Pattern

(Enlarge 200%)

Cut 2 from each fabric.
Cut 2 from lining.
Cut 2 from interfacing.

Place on fold.

skirts

BY AMY STALP

A SEWING PATTERN GIVES YOU A PRETTY GOOD PICTURE of what the finished garment will look like. But that doesn't mean that you have to make the garment as shown. It's fun to change things up and show off your style. These skirts are all made from the same pattern, and each one is a little different. Try one of these ideas or experiment with your own. Think of the basic pattern as a blank canvas, and then create your own work of art using fabric, thread, trims and more.

tropical

Instead of sewing a fabric band on the skirt lower edge, attach a funky trim for a short and sassy look.

instructions

1. To shorten the skirt, find the shorten-or-lengthen line on each pattern piece. Fold each pattern piece and reduce the length by the desired amount.

Tape or pin the pattern to secure. Trim the folded portion using a clear ruler as a guide (**A**).

2. Cut out the skirt. Construct the skirt following the pattern guidesheet.

3. Measure the skirt's hem circumference and add 1″. Purchase that amount of trim.

4. Pin the trim to the skirt hem wrong side, tucking under the ends. Stitch the trim in place (**B**).

Beaded trim adds color and style.

YOU WILL NEED:

TROPICAL

• skirt pattern (such as Kwik Sew 3337)

• fabric (yardage as indicated on pattern envelope)

• trim (See step #3 to determine the amount; the featured skirt required 2½ yards.)

• 7″ zipper

• matching all-purpose thread

A Fold, tape and trim pattern.

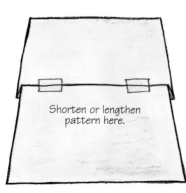

Shorten or lengthen pattern here.

B Stitch trim in place.

KWIK SEW 3337

Pleasingly Pieced

KWIK SEW 3337

Paint It Red

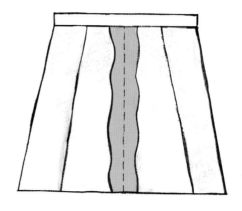

KWIK SEW 3337

pleasingly pieced

Piece together different fabrics to create this skirt. Mix a variety of prints and colors.

instructions

1. Cut each fabric into strips of varying widths. Arrange the strips, alternating widths and fabrics (**C**).

2. Right sides facing and using a ½″ seam, sew the fabric strips together along the lengthwise edges. Press open the seams.

3. Using the pieced fabric, cut out the skirt.

4. Construct the skirt following the pattern guidesheet.

paint it red

Use two different black and white print fabrics, and add some eye-catching trim.

instructions

1. Cut out the skirt as directed by the pattern guidesheet. Cut one front, side and back panel from each fabric.

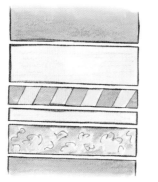

C Arrange fabric strips.

D Stitch down center of trim.

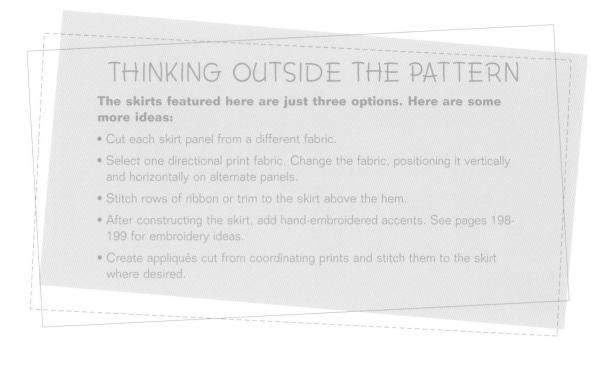

2. Construct the skirt following the pattern guidesheet, alternating the different fabric panels.

3. To determine the amount of trim needed, measure the center-front skirt seam and multiply that by 5. Measure the center-back seam from the zipper lower edge to the hem. Add the two numbers plus 12″. Purchase that amount of trim.

4. Cut five lengths of trim the length of the center-front seam plus 1″. On one trim length, turn under ¼″ on one end; turn under ¼″ again. Center the trim on the center-front seam, positioning the folded edge at the waistband

seam; pin. Turn under ¼″ on the lower end; turn under the end again, wrapping it around the hem. Pin the trim in place.

5. Stitch down the center of the trim to secure (**D**). Repeat to stitch the trim to each of the four side-panel seams. Stitch the remaining trim length to the center-back seam, positioning the upper edge just below the zipper lower edge.

SOURCE | **RJR Fabrics**, rjrfabrics.com, provided the fabric. | **Kwik Sew Patterns**, kwiksew.com, provided the pattern.

THINKING OUTSIDE THE PATTERN

The skirts featured here are just three options. Here are some more ideas:

- Cut each skirt panel from a different fabric.
- Select one directional print fabric. Change the fabric, positioning it vertically and horizontally on alternate panels.
- Stitch rows of ribbon or trim to the skirt above the hem.
- After constructing the skirt, add hand-embroidered accents. See pages 198-199 for embroidery ideas.
- Create appliqués cut from coordinating prints and stitch them to the skirt where desired.

broomstick skirt

BY SHANNON DENNIS

THIS EASY-BREEZY SKIRT IS THE PERFECT THING to slip on for a casual outing. The elastic waistband is comfortable to wear and easy to sew. Experiment with different fabrics to find the perfect combination that reflects your personality and style.

instructions

1. For the waistband tier length, measure your hips at the widest point and add 5″ to 7″ (depending on the desired fullness). The featured skirt's waistband tier measures 5″ x 50″. Cut enough 5″-wide fabric strips to measure 50″. Right sides facing, stitch two strips together along one short edge (**A**). Repeat until you have enough length to cut the waistband tier to the determined dimensions.

2. To create the waistband tier casing, turn the upper edge ¼″ to the wrong side; press. Turn the upper edge another 1″ to the wrong side; press and pin. Stitch along the lower fold using a ¼″ seam (**B**).

3. For the second tier length, multiply the waistband tier length by 1.5. The featured skirts' second tier measures 5″ x 75″. Piece together enough 5″-wide fabric strips to cut the second tier to the determined dimensions.

4. For the third tier length, multiply the second tier length by 1.5. The featured skirt's third tier measures 5″ x 112½″. Piece together enough 5″-wide fabric strips to cut the third tier to the determined dimensions.

5. For the fourth tier length, multiply the third tier length by 1.5. The featured skirt's fourth tier measures 5″ x 168¾″. Piece together enough 5″-wide fabric strips to cut the fourth tier to the determined dimensions.

6. For the fifth tier length, multiply the fourth tier length by 1.5. The featured skirt's fifth tier measures 5″ x 253⅛″. Piece together enough 5″-wide fabric strips to cut the fifth tier to the determined dimensions.

7. Set your sewing machine for a basting stitch (4.5 stitch length). Using a ½″ seam, baste the upper edge of the second tier. Leave approximately 5″-long thread tails at the beginning and end of the seam.

YOU WILL NEED:

- NOTE: Fabric amounts may change depending on your measurements. The listed amounts are for the featured skirt. See steps #1-6 to determine fabric amounts.

- ⅓ yard of fabric 1 (waistband tier)

- ⅓ yard of fabric 2 (second tier)

- ½ yard of fabric 3 (third tier)

- ⅝ yard of fabric 4 (fourth tier)

- ⅞ yard of fabric 5 (fifth tier)

- 1 yard of ¾″-wide elastic (more or less depending on waist measurement)

- matching all-purpose thread

A Stitch strips together.

B Stitch casing.

FINISHING OPTIONS

Finishing the inside of a garment is important not only for the visual effect of the garment but also for wear and tear. There are several ways to finish a seam.

A zigzag or overlock stitch on a standard sewing machine is good for light- to mediumweight fabrics. Stitch close to the fabric edge so the right-hand stitches go just off the fabric to "encase" the raw edge and prevent it from fraying.

Another finishing option is achieved with a serger. A serger can evenly stitch the seam while finishing the raw edge. You can also use a serger to hem, as shown on the featured skirt.

CUT YOUR SEWING TIME IN HALF!

If you want a faster method than gathering by hand, use a gathering foot or ruffler on your machine.

8. Ease, or gently pull, one of the threads to gather the fabric. Continue pulling the same thread; do not switch. Gather the fabric until the upper edge measures the same length as the waistband tier lower edge.

9. Right sides facing, pin the second tier's gathered edge to the waistband tier lower edge. Evenly distribute the gathers. Stitch, using a ½" seam (**C**). Zigzag-finish the seam; press open.

10. Repeat to gather and stitch the remaining tiers, evenly distributing the gathers.

11. Before measuring the elastic, determine where you want the waistband to rest. Place the elastic around your body at that place; do not pull it tight. Cut the elastic to the desired measurement.

12. Attach a safety pin or bodkin to one end of the elastic, and insert it into the casing. Pin the opposite end of the elastic to the skirt to prevent it from getting lost in the casing. Guide the elastic through the casing. Remove the pin and zigzag each end of the elastic to the skirt (**D**).

13. Right sides facing, fold the skirt lengthwise and match the raw edges; pin. Using a ½" seam, stitch the side seam (**E**). Zigzag-finish the raw edges.

14. Hem the skirt using any method you prefer. (For more information on hemming, see page 165.) The featured skirt was hemmed using a 3-thread rolled hem on a serger.

SOURCE | **RJR Fabrics**, rjrfabrics.com, provided the fabric.

C Stitch tiers 1 and 2.

D Zigzag elastic in place.

E Stitch side seam.

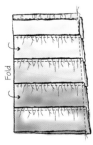

button-trimmed sweater

BY LINDA GRIEPENTROG

WHY SETTLE FOR A PLAIN SWEATER? If you can sew on a button (if you don't know how yet, go to page 173), you can easily personalize clothing and make it uniquely yours. Add as many or as few buttons as you choose—you're the designer.

instructions

1. First, consider the sweater knit—can it support the weight of many buttons and still hang properly? To prevent drooping edges, add lightweight fusible interfacing or grosgrain ribbon behind the areas where you're adding buttons.

2. Position all the buttons on the sweater before doing any stitching. Rearrange the buttons until you're happy with the design. As a general rule for lightweight sweaters, stick to buttons that are ⅝"-diameter or smaller. Look for sew-through buttons, as shank buttons may sag along the sweater edges.

3. Sew the buttons on by hand or machine.

SOURCE | **JHB International Inc.,** buttons.com, provided the buttons. E-mail sales@buttons.com to locate a retailer.

YOU WILL NEED:

• cardigan sweater

• buttons
  (⅝" or smaller)

yo-yo scarf

BY GENA BLOEMENDAAL

STRING TOGETHER A BUNCH OF YO-YOS to make a delicate yet eye-catching scarf.

instructions

1. Wash and dry the fabric to prepare it. Press out any wrinkles, and then lay the fabric right side down on a flat work surface.

2. Using a compass and fabric-marking pen, draw twenty 4″-diameter circles on each fabric piece. Cut out the circles ¼″ outside the drawn lines.

3. With a needle and strong thread, stitch each circle into a small yo-yo as instructed on page 200.

4. Place the yo-yos in piles according to their fabric and give a number (1-4) to each pile. Arrange the yo-yos in the pattern indicated using half the yo-yos (40) for each row (**A**).

5. Using just a few stitches, hand stitch the yo-yos together where they abut (**B**). Stitch each row of yo-yos, and then stitch the two rows together. Another option is to select a narrow, short zigzag stitch on your sewing machine and take a few stitches where indicated to connect the yo-yos.

A Arrange yo-yos.

B Stitch yo-yos together.

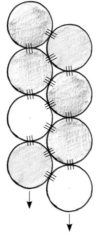

*Use fabric scraps from leftover projects to make the yo-yos. The number of fabrics listed is a guideline; choose as many or as few as you like.

pajama pants

BY AMY STALP

AFTER A LONG DAY, there's nothing better than slipping into a pair of comfy lounge pants. Whether you make them from cotton, flannel or terry cloth, these pants are sure to become your favorite.

instructions

1. Decide if you want to make full- or capri-length pants. Find a pair of pants the desired length that fit you comfortably. Measure the inseam. Lengthen or shorten the pattern, if necessary, at the horizontal adjustment line.

2. On the pants front and back pattern pieces, measure up 4″ plus the hem allowance from the lower edge and draw a line across the width of the pattern (**A**). Many patterns allow a 1¼″ hem, so you'd measure 5¼″ from the lower edge.

3. Cut across the line to create a pattern for the contrasting band. Label the pattern pieces front and back (**B**).

4. Cut two each of the front and back pant pattern pieces from the main fabric. Cut two each of the front and back band pattern pieces from the contrasting fabric.

5. Right sides together and using a ½″ seam allowance, stitch the contrasting bands to the pant legs, matching the front and back pieces (**C**).

6. Measure the width of the pant leg along the seam. Cut four ribbon pieces that length. Center a ribbon piece over each seam; stitch (**D**). Save the remaining ribbon for the drawstring.

7. Finish constructing the pants following the pattern guidesheet.

SOURCES | **Denver Fabrics**, denverfabrics.com, provided the fabrics and ribbon. | **McCall's**, mccall.com, (800) 782-0323, provided the pattern. | **Beacon Fabric & Notions**, beaconfabric.com, (800) 713-8157, provided the elastic.

YOU WILL NEED:

- pajama pants pattern
- main fabric (yardage as indicated on pattern envelope)
- ¼ yard of contrasting fabric
- ½″-wide grosgrain ribbon (enough for drawstring and hems)
- ¾″-wide elastic (yardage as indicated on pattern envelope)
- matching all-purpose thread

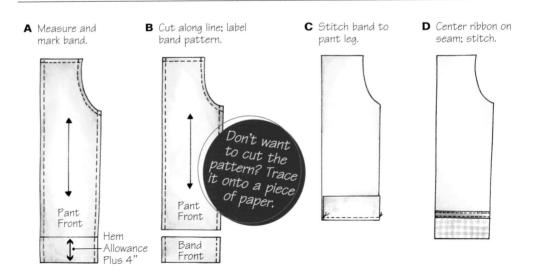

A Measure and mark band.

B Cut along line; label band pattern.

Don't want to cut the pattern? Trace it onto a piece of paper.

C Stitch band to pant leg.

D Center ribbon on seam; stitch.

Pant Front

Pant Front

Hem Allowance Plus 4″

Band Front

smock top

BY LINDA PERMANN

THIS BOLD FLORAL TOP IS A CINCH TO STITCH. A button-loop closure means even beginner sewers can give it a shot. Wear it alone or over a T-shirt for a fun bohemian look.

instructions

Use ½" seam allowances unless otherwise noted.

bodice

1. Take your high-bust measurement (or where you want to position the shirt upper edge). Add four inches to this measurement to determine the length of the contrasting band; record. Cut a rectangle of solid fabric 5½" wide by the recorded measurement for the band. Cut three 5½" x 45" solid fabric strips; set aside.

2. Fold the band in half lengthwise with right sides facing; press. If the fabric is thin, cut a strip of lightweight fusible interfacing that measures 2¼" x the band length. Fuse the interfacing to the band wrong side following the manufacturer's instructions (**A**).

3. Fold each band long edge ½" toward the wrong side; press. Fold one short end ½" toward the wrong side; press. Wrap the band around your high bust. Make sure the band fits snugly. To shorten the band for a snug fit, mark the desired placement, and then trim the band ½" longer than the mark. Fold the raw end ½" toward the wrong side; press.

4. To make the front panel, cut one 24" x 30" rectangle of print fabric on the crossgrain. Cut two 12" x 24" rectangles for the back panels. Cut each piece in the same direction so the pattern repeats match.

5. With right sides together, align one back panel long edge with one front panel short edge; pin. Using a ⅞" seam allowance, stitch the long edge; press. Repeat to stitch the remaining back panel to the opposite front panel short edge.

6. Align the back panel long edges with right sides facing; pin. Measure 13" up from the shirt lower edge; pin-mark. Stitch from the shirt lower edge to the pin mark; backstitch to secure.

A Apply interfacing.

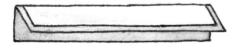

Remove the pin and baste from the mark to the shirt upper edge; don't backstitch at the end of the seam. Press open the seam. Turn under each seam allowance long edge ⅜"; press. Stitch along each fold (**B**). Remove the basting stitches using a seam ripper (**C**).

7. To hem the shirt, fold the lower edge ½" toward the wrong side; press. Fold the edge again 1" toward the wrong side; press. Stitch close to the first foldline.

8. Using a long basting stitch, stitch across the shirt upper edge. Leave long thread tails. Don't backstitch at the beginning or end of the seam.

9. Fold the band in half widthwise and pin-mark the center. Fold the ends toward the pin, and pin-mark the side folds. Gently pull the basting thread tails to gather the shirt upper edge. Position the gathered edge between the band fold (**D**). Align the shirt side seams with the band pin marks. Evenly distribute the gathers and pin them in place along the band right side. Stitch

along the band lower edge, catching the gathers. Stitch one band short end closed.

10. Sew the button to the band closed end, about 1" from the edge. Cut a 1"x 5" strip from the solid fabric. Fold the strip in half lengthwise with right sides facing. Stitch the long edge to form a tube. Turn the tube right side out; press. Wrap the tube around the button, and tuck the tube raw ends into the band pressed edge to form a button loop. Pin the loop in place, making sure it's long enough to easily button and unbutton the shirt. Stitch the band folded edge closed, making sure to catch both loop ends (**E**).

straps & sash

1. Fold each remaining 5½"x 45" strip in half lengthwise with right sides facing; press. If the fabric is thin, cut a strip of lightweight fusible interfacing 2¼" wide by the strip length. Fuse the interfacing to the fabric strips according to the manufacturer's instructions. Stitch each strip long edge; turn right side out.

Hem the shirt last if you want it shorter. Try on the shirt, mark the length, add 1½"; mark. Cut along the mark. Follow step 7.

B Stitch along each fold.

C Remove basting stitches.

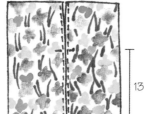

13"

D Position shirt gathered edge between band fold.

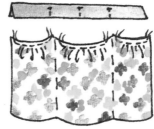

E Stitch band folded edge.

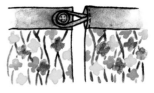

2. Cut one strip in half to make two straps. Try on the shirt, and pin the straps to the band along the front and back until the desired fit is achieved. Carefully remove the shirt. Trim the straps if necessary, and then fold in the strap short edges about ½" toward the wrong side. Adjust the strap folded edges so they align with the band lower edge and still fit correctly. Press each strap folded end; pin the strap ends along the band upper and lower edges. From the shirt right side, stitch around the band upper and lower edge, making sure to catch each strap in the stitching (**F**).

3. Fold one end of one remaining strip ½" toward the wrong side; press. Tuck one end of the second strip into the fold; pin. Stitch across the fold. Press each raw end ½" toward the wrong side; pin and stitch along the fold. Tie the sash around your waist while wearing the shirt.

SOURCE | **Reprodepot.com** provided the fabric.

F Stitch band upper and lower edges.

fabric belt

BY AMY STALP

THIS FUN ACCESSORY IS A CINCH to make. Create several belts using different fabrics—they just might become your favorite accessories.

instructions

1. To determine the length of fabric, measure your waist (or hips, depending on where you plan to wear the belt) and add 10″ to 18″ depending on the desired finished length.

2. Cut one fabric strip 7″ wide by the length determined in step 1. Fold the strip in half right sides together. Cut each short end of the strip at an angle (**A**).

3. Using a ½″ seam allowance, stitch the raw edges, leaving an opening on the long edge for turning (**B**).

4. Turn the strip right side out. Press, turning the opening raw edges to the inside ½″.

5. Slipstitch the opening closed. Or edgestitch around the entire belt, closing the opening edges with the stitches.

YOU WILL NEED:

• fabric (See step #1 to determine the length.)

• matching all-purpose thread

● ● ● ● ●

Make a reversible belt and double your options

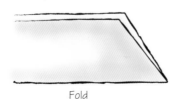

A Cut strip end at an angle.

Fold

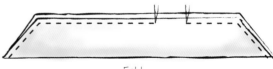

B Stitch, leaving an opening for turning.

Fold

lace-trimmed jacket

BY PAM ARCHER

BY PAM ARCHER

ADD A TOUCH OF LACE to make an everyday jacket special. Lace's open weave allows whatever lies beneath to be filtered through, altering the original fabric. Layering lace on another fabric adds texture and saturated color and increases the eye appeal—and it's sew simple to do. Try this technique on a jacket project or a ready-made garment.

To select a lace color, look closely at the fashion fabric for color tips. Examine the fabric selvages to see what colors were used to create the fabric. You may be pleasantly surprised by some new color options.

instructions

1. Cut the jacket pieces from the fabric and interfacing as directed in the pattern guidesheet.

2. From the lace, cut one collar, two pockets and two pocket flaps.

3. Using the pattern provided on the button package, cut four button covers each from the fabric and the lace.

4. On the sleeve pattern, measure 4″ from the lower edge and draw a line parallel to the sleeve hemline. Position the sleeve pattern on the lace edge aligning the drawn line with the lace scalloped edge; cut out the lace.

5. Right sides up, position the lace pieces on the right sides of each fabric pocket, pocket flap and collar; baste.

6. Construct the jacket as directed in the pattern guidesheet up to the sleeve.

7. Right sides up, position each sleeve lace piece on the right side of each sleeve, aligning the lower straight edge (**A**); stitch. Serge- or zigzag-finish the edges. Hand tack the lace upper points to the sleeve (**B**).

YOU WILL NEED:

- jacket pattern
- 1⅛ yards of 45″-wide fabric or ⅞ yard of 60″-wide fabric for jacket
- ¾ yard of 45″-wide lace with a scallop edge
- ⅜ yard of 45″-wide fusible interfacing
- all-purpose thread to match lace
- four size 4/0 (½″) snaps
- four 1⅛″ (size 45) coverable buttons
- 70/10 or 80/12 machine-sewing needle
- thread wax

A Position lace on fabric piece.

B Hand tack lace upper points.

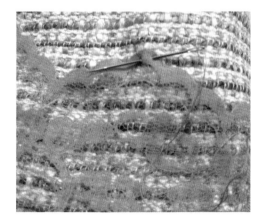

MAKE IT SNAPPY!

If making buttonholes seems daunting or you're pressed for time, consider substituting large snaps for the buttons. Snaps provide a secure closure with easy hand-sewing application. Here are some tips for successful snap sewing:

- Snaps come in a variety of sizes. When using snaps as the only closures, opt for snaps that are at least ½".

- Check the pattern for snap placement. Follow the button placement to determine where to place the snaps. Position the bust snap and adjust it to the fullest part of your bust for a secure closing. If an adjustment is required, continue to rework the remaining snap positions at equal distances.

- Before threading the needle for hand sewing, run the thread through wax. The wax strengthens the thread and keeps it straight while sewing.

- If your sewing needle is large enough, thread a second thread through the eye for double the thread coverage with one pass.

8. Continue sewing the jacket following the guidesheet.

9. Right sides up, place one lace button cover over each fabric button cover. Hand baste around the cover outer edges for even fitting. Cover the buttons following the manufacturer's instructions.

10. Optional: For fast and secure closures, use large-size snaps instead of buttonholes. Sew each button in place as the pattern directs and sew a large snap directly underneath to secure.

SOURCE | **Vogue Patterns,** (800) 782-0323, voguepatterns.com, donated the pattern.

Wings Appliqué

(Enlarge 125%)

Instructions on page 114,
reverse pattern for second wing.

jean jacket

BY SHANNON DENNIS

JEAN JACKETS ARE ALWAYS FUN, but you can make yours an original by adding reverse appliqué. Use the design provided, or create your own. For an interesting fabric source, follow our example by recycling a man's shirt for the fabric and cuffs.

instructions

1. Select your design (such as the wings on page 113). If you create your own, make sure it fits on the area you're embellishing. It should be an open design so you can cut it away and the fabric behind will show.

2. Trace the design onto the jacket right side with the fabric marking pen. On the jacket wrong side, lightly spray the temporary spray adhesive. Position the fabric right side down on the adhesive. Make sure that the decorative fabric covers the entire design area and extends at least 1″ beyond it.

3. Install the jean or stretch needle in your sewing machine. Thread the machine with matching thread in the top and the bobbin. Select a straight stitch, or use a zigzag for a bolder line.

4. On the jacket right side, stitch along the traced lines. When finished, use appliqué scissors to clip away the denim fabric outside of the shapes as shown on the featured jacket. Or, you can cut out the fabric from the inside of the shapes for a different design. Both options look great. Trim away any excess decorative fabric on the jacket wrong side. Fray the denim around the shapes as desired.

5. To make the decorative cuffs, cut the cuffs off of a ready-to-wear shirt. Center one cuff on one jacket sleeve lower edge, with the cuff right side facing the jacket wrong side. Using a ¼″ seam allowance, stitch the cuff to the jacket sleeve.

6. Turn the cuff to the jacket right side; press. Topstitch ½″ from the seamed edge. Repeat to attach the second cuff.

vintage scroll jeans

BY SHANNON DENNIS

YOU DON'T NEED A HIGH-TECH EMBROIDERY MACHINE to make an amazing pair of designer jeans. With these techniques you'll be scheduling runway shows in no time.

instructions

1. Cut out several motifs from the fabric, and position them on the jeans. Reposition the motifs until you're happy with the placement.

2. Spray the motif wrong sides with temporary spray adhesive. Reposition the motifs on the jeans; pin.

3. Remove the accessory tray of the sewing machine to create a free arm. Drop the feed dogs to set up the machine for free-motion stitching, and select a zigzag stitch. Make sure you have the appropriate foot on the machine, such as a darning foot or an open-toe foot.

4. Slide the leg of the jeans onto the sewing-machine free arm. Stitch around each motif to appliqué it to the jeans.

Note: If your jeans are a size 5 or smaller or if they have tapered legs with a skinny ankle, open up part of the inner leg seam to get the jeans on the machine. You may also need to open up part of the inner leg seam if your machine doesn't have a free arm feature.

5. Position the metallic thread on the motifs to create vines; fuse in place following the manufacturer's instructions.

6. Embellish the motifs with crystals, following the manufacturer's instructions.

YOU WILL NEED:

- ¼ to ¾ yard of printed fabric with motifs you can cut out
- jeans
- matching or contrasting cotton thread
- temporary spray adhesive (such as KK2000)
- seam ripper
- fusible metallic ribbon
- fusible crystals
- optional: crystal applicator

jean-eology

bangle bag

BY LISA SHEPARD STEWART

THIS PROJECT IS LIKE TWO ACCESSORIES IN ONE. The handles are bracelets, so you can wear the bag on your wrist and keep your hands free. So find a pair of bangles you love, find fabric to match, and start stitching.

Finished size: approximately 6"x 8"

instructions

1. Cut two 3½" squares from the main fabric and the interfacing for the tabs. Fuse the interfacing to the fabric wrong sides following the manufacturer's instructions. Fold two tab edges toward the interfacing side so they overlap and the tab measures 1½" wide (**A**). Secure with hand or machine stitching, fabric glue or fusible tape. Repeat to create the second tab.

2. Wrap one tab around each bangle with the seam facing the inside. Using a zipper foot, stitch through both layers of the tab ¼" from the bangle outer edge. Trim the tab ends to ¼" (**B**).

3. Pin-mark the center of the bag upper edge and ½" from each side. Center the tabs between the pins, aligning the raw edges; baste (**C**).

4. Turn under ¼" toward the wrong side on each 10" edge of the lining rectangle; press. Right sides facing, pin the lining and main-fabric

YOU WILL NEED:

- 10"x15" rectangle of main fabric (See "Fabric Facts," right.)
- 10"x15" rectangle of lining fabric (See "Fabric Facts.")
- fusible knit interfacing
- 2 bangles
- 1 magnetic snap closure (optional)
- fabric glue (optional)

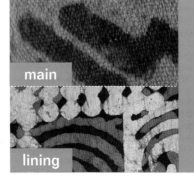

main

lining

FABRIC FACTS

To give the featured bag cultural style, use the following fabrics, which are available at culturedexpressions.com.:

Main fabric—Bogolan (mudcloth), a handwoven, hand-dyed cotton from Mali, West Africa

Lining fabric—African cotton print fabric

A Fold in tab edges.

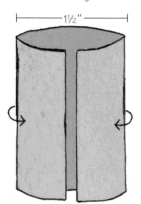

1½"

B Stitch tab; trim end.

C Center tabs; baste.

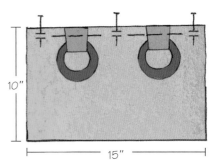

10"

15"

rectangle together along the upper edge. Stitch using a ½" seam, beginning and ending ½" from each side. Use a zipper foot to stitch close to the bangles. Open the seam; press the seam toward the lining. Understitch the seam through both the lining and the seam allowance, leaving ½" unstitched at each side edge; press (**D**). Understitching prevents the lining from rolling over the bag upper edge.

5. Right sides facing, pin the main-fabric and lining rectangles together along the lower edge. Stitch using a ½" seam, beginning and ending ½" from each side edge. Turn the bag right side out; press. Right sides facing, pin only the main fabrics together at the side edge; stitch using a ½" seam (**E**). Press open the seam, using steam to flatten the bulk. Align the lining pressed edges

to conceal the main side seam, slighlty overlapping the lining edges. Hand stitch the lining using small close stitches. Turn the bag right side out.

6. With the lining right sides facing, pin the bag lower edge. Stitch through all layers using a ¼" seam, carefully reinforcing the stitching through the bulk of the corners.

7. Reinforce the stitching across the bag upper edge at the tabs about ¼" from bag edge (**F**).

8. Optional: Attach magnetic snap closures to the inside of the bag, just below the bangle tabs.

RESOURCES | This project is adapted from Lisa's book *African Accents On The Go! Designing Accessories with Cultural Style.* **Cultured Expressions,** culturedexpressions.com, (866) 683-2568, carries the book and the bogolan fabric used in the featured bag.

D Understitch lining.

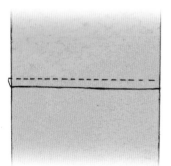

E Stitch side seam.

F Reinforce stitching.

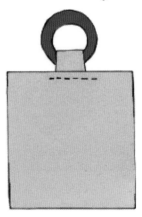

d-ring keychain

BY BETH BRADLEY

YOU WILL NEED:

- mediumweight cotton fabric
- 1⅛"-wide ribbon
- matching or contrasting all-purpose thread
- 1⅜"-wide metal D-ring
- metal key ring
- sewing machine zipper foot

• • • • •

USE LEFTOVER FABRIC, RIBBONS AND TRIM TO make a keychain to match every handbag.

instructions

Use a ¼" seam allowance.

1. Cut a 4"x 7" fabric rectangle. Cut a 7" length of ribbon.

2. Fold the fabric rectangle in half lengthwise with right sides facing; press. Stitch along the long raw edge.

3. Turn the rectangle right side out; press flat. Center the ribbon on the rectangle; pin. Edgestitch the ribbon long edges.

4. Fold the rectangle in half widthwise with right sides facing. Slip one rectangle short end through the D-ring; slide it down to the rectangle fold. Stitch across the rectangle short ends to create a loop. Turn the loop right side out.

5. Slide the D-ring to the seam end. Install a zipper foot on the sewing machine. Stitch across the rectangle width as close as possible to the D-ring, making sure to backstitch at the beginning and end of the stitching.

6. Attach the keyring to the D-ring.

SOURCE | **Strano Designs**, stranodesigns.com, provided the 1½" Fia ribbon.

Skip the ribbon and instead use a decorative stitch or monogram to decorate the fabric.

java jacket

BY PAM ARCHER

DRESS UP YOUR MORNING CUP WITH A SLEEVE that makes a fashion statement and enhances your coffee experience. Want to add something extra to your morning jolt? Expand your sewing skills by adding funky trim or an exterior pocket.

instructions

1. Prewash the fashion fabric and lining. Follow the manufacturer's instructions for laundering needle-punched insulated lining.

2. Using the pattern on page 126, cut one sleeve each from the fashion fabric, cotton batting and lining.

3. Baste the batting (or insulated lining) to the fashion fabric sleeve wrong side along each edge. Trim the batting close to the stitching line.

4. With right sides facing, pin the fashion fabric and the lining sleeves together. Using a ½" seam allowance, stitch along the long edges and one short end. With pinking sheers or a pinking blade attached to a rotary cutter, pink close to the seams.

5. Turn the sleeve right side out; press.

6. Fold under the raw short ends ¼"; press. Edgestitch along the folded edge.

7. With right sides together, align the short ends and pin. Using a ¼" seam allowance, stitch to form a center seam. Edgestitch along both sides of the center seam, catching the seam allowances in the stitching.

8. Edgestitch the upper and lower sleeve edges.

SOURCE | **The Warm Company,** (425) 248-2424, warmcompany.com, provided the Warm and Natural Cotton Batting and Insul-Bright insulation.

To trim the seam and remove excess bulk along curves, use pinking shears or a rotary cutter with a pinking blade.

YOU WILL NEED:

- 6"x12" rectangle each of fashion fabric and prequilted lining

- 6"x12" rectangle each of cotton batting or needle-punched insulated lining (if not using a prequilted lining fabric)

- size 70/10 or 80/12 needle

- matching thread

- optional: ¼ yard of coordinating ball fringe

- optional: at least a 4" square of coordinating pocket fabric

IT'S EASY BEING GREEN

Aside from being cute, this java jacket is reusable so you can help the environment while drinking your latté. Slide the jacket over a paper coffee cup and stop throwing away those cardboard sleeves.

And for all your coffee loving friends, a coffee shop gift card tucked into the pocket of the java jacket makes an excellent gift.

ADD A SHOT OF...
FRINGE

Opt for a shot of ball fringe to add a gourmet touch.

1. Prepare the coffee sleeve following steps one through three on page 122.

2. Pin the ball fringe to the wrong side of one sleeve lower edge. Position the fringe so the header aligns with the seamline and the balls lay on the sleeve. Baste the fringe in place (**1**).

3. Complete the sleeve following steps four through eight. As you turn the coffee sleeve right side out the ball fringe hangs in place.

MAKE MINE EXTRA HOT!

If you prefer your beverage steaming hot, here are a few options for keeping the heat under wraps while staying green at the same time. Consider using natural cotton batting with ironing-board insulation, needle-punched insulated or prequilted fabric. Each will provide the required insulation to buffer the heat.

- Both cotton batting and prequilted fabrics can be pre-washed along with the coffee sleeve fabric to assure uniform wash-and-wear performance (**1**).

- Needle-punched insulated lining offers added body and heat resistance. It can be machine laundered but requires no prewashing (**2**).

- Ironing-board insulation, found in home decorator departments, has a shiny side and a flat side (**3**). Generally, the shiny side is placed toward the heat, preventing it from transferring through the fabric. Check the end of the insulation bolt for specific information. Ironing-board insulation provides the least weight and bulk.

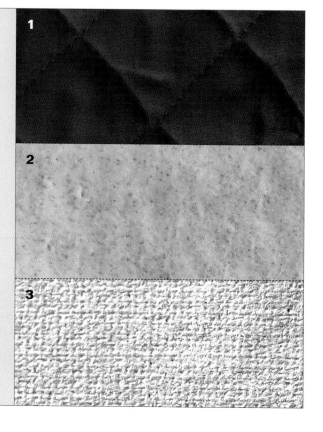

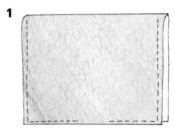

PERKY POCKET

1. Make the fabric sleeve following steps one through six on page 122.

2. From the coordinating fabric, cut one pocket from the pattern on page 126.

3. Fold the pocket in half lengthwise and use a ½" seam allowance to stitch along the two sides; leave 2" along the lower edge free. Trim the seam allowance to ¼" (**1**).

4. Turn in the lower edge ½" and press. Turn the pocket right side out and press along the upper fold and seamlines.

5. Center the pocket on the sleeve right side. Pin, and then edgestitch along the sides and lower edge.

6. Complete the sleeve following steps seven and eight on page 122.

Java Jacket Patterns

Place on fold.

Coffee Sleeve

Cut 1 from fabric.
Cut 1 from lining.
Cut 1 from insulation.

Place on fold.

Coffee Sleeve Pocket

Cut 1.

diva dress bottle bags

BY SUSAN COUSINEAU

GET THE PARTY STARTED by sewing up these fabulously feminine bottle bags. They make perfect favors for a girls' night wine or cocktail celebration. Add girly flair with pretty ribbons, appliqués, sequins, tassels or beaded trim.

instructions

Use ¼" seam allowances.

1. From the fabric, cut a 6½" x 31" rectangle using the rotary cutter, mat and ruler.

2. Fold the rectangle short edges ½" toward the wrong side; press. Cut two 6½"-long pieces of fusible tape. Insert the tape between each fold; fuse following the manufacturer's instructions.

3. Position the fabric rectangle right side up with one short edge as the upper edge. With the fabric-marking pen, draw a horizontal line on the fabric 5" down from the upper edge.

4. Center the ribbon on the fabric right side along the drawn line; pin. Stitch across the ribbon center for 2" to secure it to the fabric (**A**).

5. Fold the rectangle in half widthwise with right sides facing; press. Pin the fabric layers together along the long edges, making sure the ribbon remains inside the layers.

6. Stitch the long edges (**B**). Turn the bag right side out and press.

YOU WILL NEED:

- ¼ yard of printed cotton fabric
- ⅜"-wide fusible adhesive tape (such as Heat 'n Bond Iron-On Adhesive Hem)
- 27" of ½"- to ⅝"-wide ribbon
- 14" piece of ½"- to ⅝"-wide ribbon
- 13" of pom-pom, tassel or beaded trim
- rotary cutter and mat
- clear grid ruler
- matching all-purpose thread
- fabric-marking pen
- assorted embellishments (such as sequins, appliqués, etc.)

● ● ● ● ● ●

A Stitch across ribbon center.

5"

B Stitch side edges.

Tuck pieces of tissue paper into the bag to give the bag shape and support. For extra stability on lightweight fabric, apply fusible interfacing before sewing.

BEST DRESSED

- When choosing fabric for the Diva Dress Bottle Bags, take inspiration from seasons and holidays. For example, use plush velvet with faux fur for a Christmas cocktail party dress.

- Use the bags to wrap non-alcoholic gifts, such as bubble bath or bottled gourmet food products. You may need to adjust the dimensions of the bag to accommodate different size bottles.

- If you're getting married, these bottle bags make a great gift for your bridesmaids. Use leftover fabric from their dresses and tuck a bottle of bubbly inside. Or delight a bride-to-be with a miniature version of her dress.

- Look for price tags with string ties at the office supply store. Write the name of each recipient on a tag and pin it to the dress for a personal touch.

- Host a "Pretty in Pink" fundraising party to help in the fight against breast cancer. Ask each guest to design her own special pink dress bag with a bottle of wine inside. Then auction off the bags of wine and donate the proceeds to a local breast health center.

Invest in a rotary cutter and mat. These tools make it much easier to cut straight, even edges

7. Cut the 14″ ribbon in half to create the bag straps. Fold each ribbon piece in half. At the bag front and back upper corners, stitch each ribbon end right side to the bag wrong side (**C**).

8. Stitch the trim around the bag upper-edge opening (**D**). Stitch any additional trims and embellishments to the bag as desired.

C Stitch ribbon straps to bag.

D Stitch trim around upper edge.

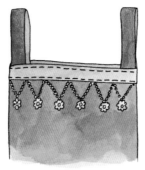

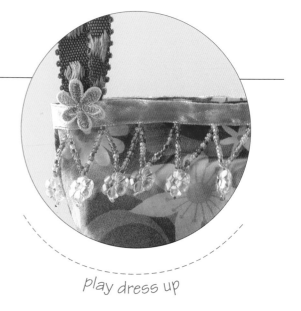

play dress up

denim pencil carrier

BY SHEILA ZENT

A GOOD PAIR OF JEANS HAS MANY LIVES, from stiff and new to distressed with holes. Even when you can no longer wear them, this wardrobe workhorse still doesn't give up. Cut apart the front and back of a pair and recycle this favorite fabric into a school accessory.

YOU WILL NEED:

- one old pair of jeans with front and back of the legs in good shape
- 12″-long zipper in contrasting color, 1″ wide
- all-purpose threads to match denim and zipper
- contrasting thread for topstitching

● ● ● ● ●

instructions

All seams are ½″ unless otherwise indicated.

1. Cut an old pair of jeans apart along the inseams and outer seams to get two flat panels of denim. Cut the following pieces with the longest edge parallel to the length of the pant legs: 3″x12″ buttonhole band, 6¼″x12″ front, 1¾″x12″ front, 8″x12″ back.

2. With right sides together, fold the buttonhole band in half lengthwise and stitch the ends. Trim off the excess fabric at each corner and turn the band right side out; press. Staystitch along

the raw edges. In the center of the band, mark the placement for a ½″-long horizontal buttonhole ¼″ from the folded edge. Mark additional buttonholes 4¼″ above and below the center mark (**A**). With contrasting thread, stitch the buttonholes according to the operator's manual for your sewing machine.

3. With right sides together, center and stitch one long edge of the zipper to the long edge of the front using a ¼″ seam allowance. The zipper will be longer than the band. Stitch the front piece of denim to the opposite edge of the zipper. Press the seam allowances toward the denim. With a contrasting thread, topstitch through all the fabric layers just outside of the zipper seams. At the top and bottom of the zipper, stitch across the zipper teeth to anchor the two sides together, being sure the zipper pull is below the stitching. Trim the ends of the zipper even with the fabric pieces (**B**).

A Mark buttonholes.

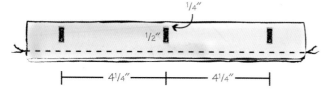

B Trim zipper ends.

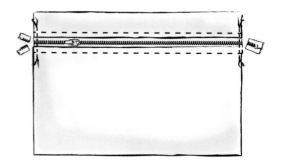

SHOW OFF

If the contrasting thread color doesn't show up well against the denim:

- Set your machine to an extra long stitch.
- Sew two rows of stitching, one on top of the other.
- Set your machine to a long stretch stitch.
- Use extra-strong denim topstitching thread.

4. With right sides together, center the buttonhole band on the long edge opposite the zipper on the front. Stitch. Open the zipper several inches. Place the back piece on the front piece right sides together with the buttonhole band sandwiched between the layers. Stitch around the outside edges, being careful not to catch the top and bottom ends of the buttonhole band. Clip the excess fabric of the seam allowances at each corner. Turn right side out through the zipper opening. Press all the edges.

5. With contrasting thread, topstitch ¼" around the outside edges of the front and back pieces (not the buttonhole band). Press.

6. Optional: Decorate the carrier with appliqués, paint or other embellishments.

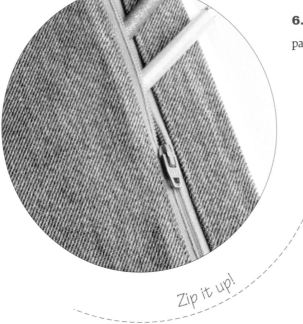

Zip it up!

Beach Ball Pattern

Cut 2 from each fabric.
Instructions on page 134.

Enlarge the pattern 400%
to create a very large beach
ball and use it as a pillow.
Purchase ½ yard each of the
three coordinating fabrics and
use the same instructions.

beach balls

BY TANYA WHELAN

BRING THE FUN AND SUN INSIDE BY MAKING FABRIC BEACH BALLS. Give away the balls to use as toys, use the balls as decorations, or attach a string loop for a keychain or ornament.

instructions

1. Copy the beach ball pattern on page 133 using a photocopier or tracing paper. For a large ball, enlarge the pattern 120%; for a small ball, scale down the pattern 90%. Or use the pattern as is for a medium-sized ball.

2. Using the pattern, cut two beach ball sections from each fabric.

3. Using a ¼" seam allowance, stitch two contrasting fabrics together along one long edge with right sides facing. Backstitch securely at the beginning and end of each seam.

4. Stitch another contrasting fabric to the joined piece with right sides facing and along one long edge. Press open all seams (**A**).

5. Repeat to sew the remaining three ball sections, arranging the pieces in the same sequence as for the previous half of the ball.

6. With right sides facing, stitch the two halves together along the perimeter. Leave a 1½" opening along one long edge for stuffing.

7. Stuff the ball with cotton batting, shaping as you go to ensure a symmetrical shape.

8. Whipstitch or slipstitch the opening closed using a hand-sewing needle.

YOU WILL NEED:

(makes one large beach ball)

- 1 fat quarter each of three coordinating cotton fabrics
- cotton batting or stuffing
- coordinating all-purpose thread
- hand-sewing needle

Combine different patterns, such as stripes, dots and a floral or a damask, for a cool yet coordinated effect.

A Press open seams.

dog bed

BY HEATHER BERRY

SPEND AN AFTERNOON MAKING A DURABLE, COMFORTABLE AND WASHABLE TOSS-PILLOW BED FOR YOUR POOCH. The best part is that if you make a mistake, Fido probably won't hold it against you.

instructions

Use ½″ seam allowances unless otherwise noted.

1. Right sides facing, pin the fabric A rectangles together. Stitch around the perimeter, leaving a 2″ opening on one long side for turning (**A**). Clip the corners. Press open the seam allowances.

2. Turn the rectangle right side out. Stuff it with fiberfill. Slipstitch the opening closed.

3. Cut one fabric B rectangle long edge with pinking shears, trimming off ¼″. Fold the pinked edge 1″ toward the wrong side; press. Stitch a ½″ hem. Repeat for the other B rectangle.

4. Position the fabric B rectangles right side up so that one hemmed edge overlaps the other by 3½″. Baste the rectangles together at the overlap (**B**).

5. Right sides facing, pin the fabric B rectangles to the fabric C rectangle. Stitch around the perimeter. Clip the corners. Turn the rectangle right side out. Place the pillow inside the cover.

YOU WILL NEED:

(fits a 40 to 70 pound dog)

- two 34″x44″ rectangles of light-weight cotton fabric, such as muslin or sheeting (fabric A)
- two 20″x44″ rectangles of washable corduroy fabric (fabric B)
- 34″x44″ rectangle of heavyweight washable fabric, such as denim or fleece (fabric C)
- 2 to 3 pounds of washable cotton or polyester fiberfill
- coordinating all-purpose or upholstery thread
- pinking shears

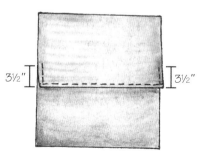

EXTRA, EXTRA

Add a personal touch so your dog can relax in style.

- Cut craft felt in the shape of a dog bone, monogram, etc. and stitch it in place.
- Make a different bed cover for each season or holiday using festive printed fabric.
- Use leftover fabric to make your dog a matching bandanna or stuffed toy.

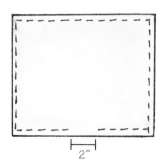

A Stitch around perimeter.

2″

B Baste rectangles together.

3½″   3½″

✳ Instead of muslin, use recycled bed sheets for the pillowcase.

shopping for a machine

SEWING MACHINES RANGE from the very basic and affordable to models with lots of bells and whistles for considerably more money. You'll find machines for sale at discount stores, as well as at stores that specialize in selling sewing machines, called machine dealerships. Machine dealers usually sell only one or two different machine brands (such as Bernina, Baby Lock, Husqvarna Viking, Elna, Janome, Brother, etc.), and are very knowledgeable about those machines.

If you're shopping for a new sewing machine, think about what kind of sewing you plan to do and how much you plan to use the machine. Also think about what kinds of sewing you might want to try. Start by talking with friends and family who own machines. Ask them what they like and dislike about their machines. Then visit a local machine dealer. Talk to them about different models. Take a few minutes and try sewing on each machine, making sure to sew a variety of fabrics to rate the machine's performance. Experiment with buttonholes and specialty stitches. Try different machine features or have the dealer explain and demonstrate the features for you.

If you plan on only doing basic sewing, the machine must have: straight stitch, reverse stitching, zigzag stitch, buttonhole feature (preferably one-step) and a zipper foot.

If you plan on sewing home-dec projects, the machine must be able to sew both heavyweight and sheer fabrics.

If you want to do quilting and free-motion embroidery, look for a machine with the ability to drop the feed dogs, and that has a ¼″ presser foot and quilting guides, built-in decorative and quilt stitches, and an embroidery foot or darning foot.

If you plan to embroider digitized designs, you'll need a machine that does both sewing and embroidery.

When you do purchase a machine, take advantage of the classes offered by the dealer. Many dealers offer free classes that will help you learn how to use your machine and get the most out of it. As a machine owner, the two most important relationships to develop are with your dealer and with your owner's manual. Both of these resources are there to help you, so utilize them whenever necessary.

If you take good care of your machine, it will treat you well in return. Have your machine serviced at least once a year by a professional. The dealer who sold you the machine will be able to recommend someone if they don't have a maintenance person on staff.

The most important thing you can do when you get your new machine home is take it out of the box and start using it as soon as possible. Whether you spend some time experimenting with the different features on scrap fabric or you jump right into a project, the sooner you start using the machine, the better.

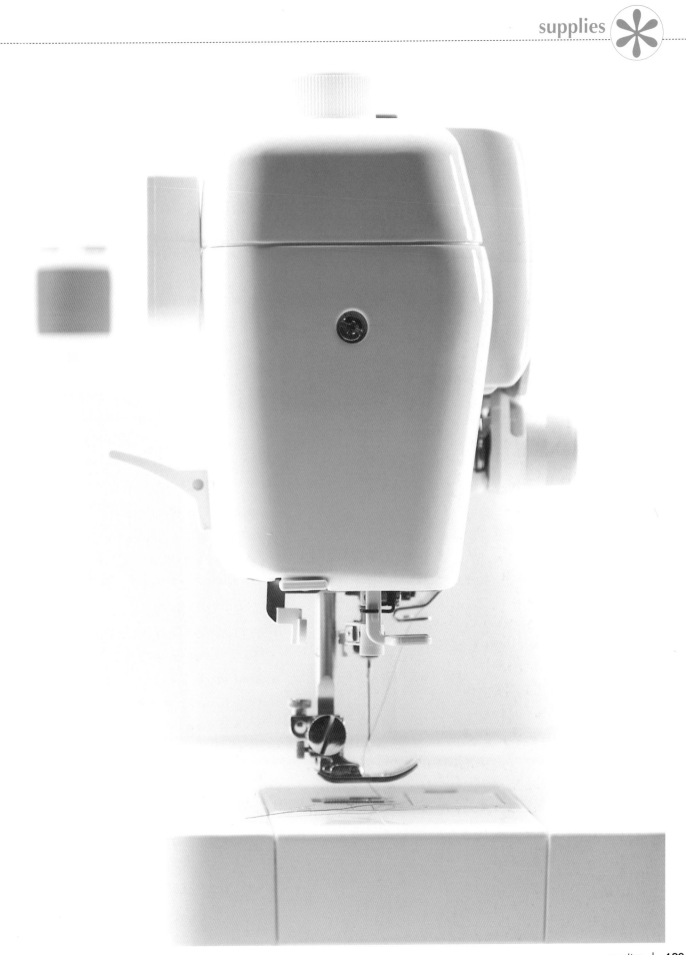

tools you will need

measuring

Transparent Rulers—allow you to see what you're measuring. Accurate horizontal and vertical lines are a must when measuring and cutting with a rotary cutter and mat (**1**).

Tape Measures—are useful for aligning the fabric grainline and for taking your body measurements to determine pattern size. Choose one made from material that won't stretch, yet bends easily around the body (**2**).

Seam Gauge—is a 6″ ruler that has a double-pointed, movable slide. It helps make accurate measurements quickly, and is useful for measuring seam allowance widths, hems and more (**3**).

marking

Fabric-Marking Pens—come in air- and water-soluble forms. Air-soluble inks disappear with time. Water-soluble inks need to be washed away with water. Test markers before using them on your project fabric; some are permanently set by heat. When purchasing markers, read the packaging carefully to determine their intended use and to make sure they're temporary (**4**).

Marking Chalk—is available in several forms: pencil, as powder in a rolling wheel dispenser or in a firm triangular shape with beveled edges. Chalk marks are easily erased from most fabrics (**5**).

Narrow Masking Tape—is a marking option when other methods are less suitable.

Tracing Wheel and Paper—Tracing paper has a colored surface that transfers to fabric when you roll over it with a tracing wheel. It comes in a variety of colors and is either water-soluble or waxed. Water-soluble marks are easily removed with a damp cloth. Choose the lightest color paper possible that's visible on the fabric in case the markings don't come out. A serrated or sawtooth wheel is most commonly used, but a smooth wheel is preferable on delicate fabrics (**6**).

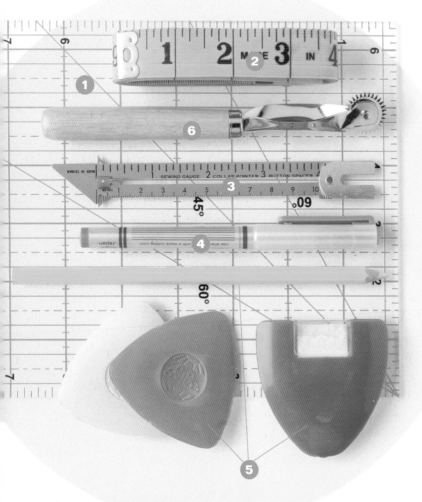

cutting

Bent Dressmaker Shears—are one of the best choices for sewing. The 8″ length is good for smooth cutting along pattern lines or long, clean fabric cuts. Extremely sharp blades make cutting easier no matter what the fabric weight or how many layers. A bend of about 45° at the pivot point lets the entire lower blade glide along the cutting table. This adds stability and allows the fabric to lie flatter when cutting (**7**).

Sewing Scissors—have blades less than 6″ long. Use them mainly for clipping threads and trimming seams (**8**).

Seam Ripper—is used for removing stitches. It has a sharp point that slides under the stitches and cuts the thread (**9**).

Rotary Cutter—looks and works like a pizza cutter. For safety purposes, remember to cover or lock the blade when not in use. Use a rotary cutter with a cutting mat, which protects your work surface (**10**).

Pinking Shears and Pinking Rotary Cutters— are used to finish seams. They cut a zigzag or scalloped edge rather than a straight line (**11**).

pressing

Steam Iron—a good steam iron is the most important pressing tool. Choose one that allows you to control the amount of steam, ranging from no steam to a heavy burst of steam (**12**).

Ironing Surface—a firmly padded, sturdy, cotton-covered ironing surface is needed, whether it's an ironing board, table or portable board. Steam needs to pass through the fabric and ironing surface.

Press Cloths or Soleplate Attachments—help to prevent shine when pressing on the fabric right side. For best results, press cloths should be made from natural fibers, such as cotton or wool (**13**).

Seam Roll—this stuffed fabric tube is used to press straight seams to prevent the seam allowances from being imprinted on the fabric right side. It's also helpful when pressing sleeve and pant-leg seams. (**14**).

Pressing Ham—duplicates body curves. Pressing over this round object instead of a flat ironing surface builds in three-dimensional shape (**15**).

sewing

Sewing Machine Needles—come in a variety of styles and sizes. The correct needle choice depends mostly on the type of fabric you're using. Universal needles are suitable for both woven and knit fabrics. Stretch needles gently spread knit fibers apart rather than piercing them. Denim/ sharp needles are designed to pierce tightly woven
fabrics. The size of the needle is usually given in both European (70, 75, 80) and American (10, 11, 12) numbering systems. Use the smaller numbers for lightweight fabrics and larger numbers for heavyweight fabrics (**16**).

Twin Sewing Machine Needles—consist of two needles on one shank, and sew parallel lines of stitches. They're useful for hemming knits. Before using a twin needle, make sure the hole in the throat plate of your sewing machine is large enough to accommodate it (**17**).

Hand-Sewing Needles—also come in a variety of sizes and styles. Sharps, which have round eyes and sharp points, are commonly used for general-purpose hand sewing. Ballpoint needles have a rounded point that pushes between fabric fibers rather than piercing them, making them perfect for sewing knits. Crewels are sharp, large-eyed medium-length needles, designed for embroidery (**18**).

Thread—is available in many different types, such as all-purpose, cotton, silk, machine embroidery, metallic and more. All-purpose thread is appropriate for most fabrics. If you're just beginning to sew, all-purpose thread is a good choice for your projects (**19**).

Straight Pins—come in a variety of lengths and diameters. For basic sewing, use pins with colored ball heads—they're easier to see and pick up (**20**).

Pincushions—store your pins. The most popular version is the stuffed tomato-shaped pincushion. You'll also find magnetic pincushions that attract and hold steel pins (**21**).

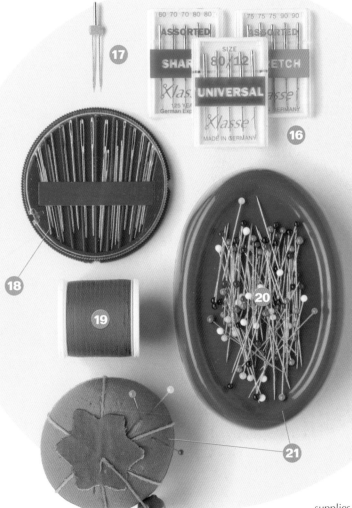

special products

Elastics—come in a variety of widths and styles. Purchase elastic by the yard or in precut packages (**22**).

Bodkin—is used to thread elastic or cording through a casing (**23**).

Point Turner—has a pointed end for pushing out corners, such as inside a pillow cover or a collar (**24**).

Beeswax—helps prevent thread from tangling and knotting when hand sewing. Pull the thread length through the beeswax once or twice (**25**).

Seam Sealant—is a colorless liquid that prevents fraying or raveling by slightly stiffening the fabric. It's also helpful for reinforcing buttonholes. Make sure to test the sealant before using it to verify that the liquid won't discolor the fabric (**26**).

Buttonhole Cutter & Block—are handy tools for accurately cutting buttonhole centers. The wooden block protects your work surface (**27**).

SOURCES | **Hemline Notions** and **Madeira Retail Products,** distributed by **SCS, Sewing & Craft Supply, USA,** (800) 547-8025, info@scsusa1.com | **Martelli Enterprises,** (850) 433-1414, martellinotions.com | **Nancy's Notions,** (800) 833-0690, nancysnotions.com | **ThreadArt,** (800) 504-6867, threadart.com | **YLI Corporation,** (803) 985-3100, ylicorp.com | These companies provided the tools and notions.

KNOW YOUR NEEDLES

Choosing the right needle makes stitching easier and gives better results. There's a needle designed for every type of sewing, quilting and needlework project. Hand needles vary by length, size, point and eye shape. When selecting a needle size, the higher the number, the finer the needle. For example, a size 9 needle is finer than a size 7. The needle size you need is determined by the thickness of the thread, embroidery floss or yarn and the thickness of the fabric.

Use these guidelines for selecting the type of needle.

1. Appliqué—short, very fine needles for hand appliqué and detailed sewing on delicate fabrics.

2. Sharps—general-purpose sewing needles for hemming and sewing on buttons. Use a size 7 for mediumweight fabrics and size 9 for sheer light-weight fabrics.

3. Embroidery—needles with long eyes for embroidery, ribbon embroidery, crewel work and general sewing. Embroidery needles are the same as Sharps, but they have longer eyes to accommodate embroidery floss, ribbon and yarn.

4. Quilting—sometimes called betweens. These needles are very short, very fine and have round eyes. A size 7 or 8 is recommended for beginners; a size 12 is for seasoned quilters. The shorter length makes it easier to form small quilting stitches.

5. Leather—These needles have a sharp triangular point designed to pierce leather, suede and some plastics without tearing.

6. Easy-Threading—Ideal for those who have difficulty threading a needle, these needles (Calyx-eye Sharps) have a slotted eye. The thread is pulled into the slotted eye; the lower eye simply provides the spring.

7. Chenille—large-eye needles with sharp points for crewel embroidery, ribbon embroidery and tying quilts.

8. Tapestry—large-eye needles with blunt points for needlepoint, counted cross-stitch, ribbon embroidery and for stitching knotted or crocheted projects.

9. Tapestry Petites—short, large-eye needles with blunt points. The shorter length makes them easy to manipulate.

10. Bead Embroidery Sharp Point—very fine, short needles used for beaded embroidery and for stitching on paper when making greeting cards.

11. Beading—very fine, long needles with long eyes for stringing beads and sewing beads on fabric.

12. Cotton Darners—long needles with sharp points and long eyes for hand basting quilt layers and mending.

13. Yarn Darners—long needles with large eyes and sharp points for soft sculpture, mending, darning and stitching with yarn.

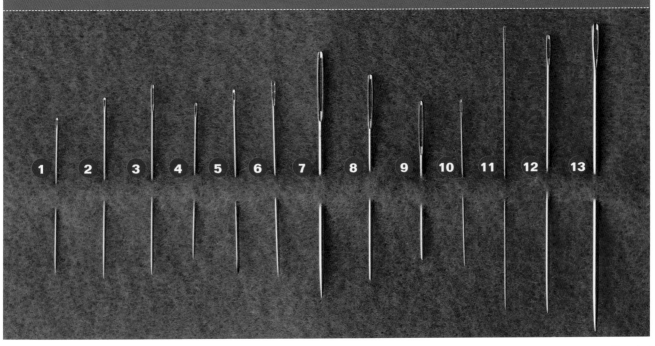

fabric

SELECTING FABRIC FOR YOUR PROJECT can be fun, but it can also be a daunting task. The variety of fabrics available can overwhelm you, but not after you take this crash course. These basic guidelines will help you choose the best fabric for each project, and make shopping fun—just as it should be.

put it to use

Before buying fabric for a project, think about its intended use. What sort of quality do you desire? Are you aiming for a casual or dressy look? Will current fashion or home-dec trends affect the selection? If the fabric is for a garment, will you wear it when it's cooler or during the heat of the day? Is the garment for winter, spring, summer or fall? If the fabric is for a home-dec project, is there a color scheme or mood you have in mind? Do you like textured or smooth surfaces? Are you more drawn to solids or prints? Do you need a fabric that can be washed frequently? Answer these questions to begin narrowing down your choices and identify the required fabric type.

fiber content

Natural-fiber fabrics are made from materials that grow in nature—examples include cotton, linen, silk, wool and rayon.

Synthetic fabrics are made from manmade fibers—examples include polyester, acrylic, acetate and spandex.

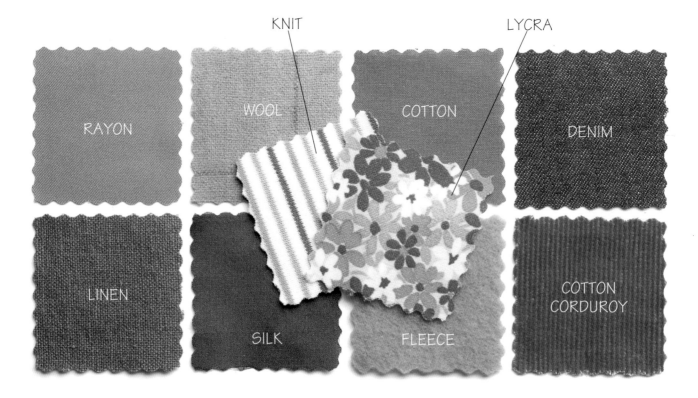

Fabric blends are combinations of two or more fibers. They offer the characteristics and best qualities of each fiber.

fabric structure

Woven fabrics are made of lengthwise and crosswise fibers that are woven together. The outer edges of woven fabrics are the selvages. The diagonal—or bias—has the most stretch.

Knit fabrics are made of rows of interlocking yarn loops. All knit fabrics stretch, some more than others. Patterns designed for knit fabrics have a stretch gauge on the envelope. Fold over the crosswise edge of the fabric about 3″ from the cut end. Hold 4″ of the folded fabric edge against the chart and gently stretch to the outer line. If the fabric stretches easily without excessive rolling to the outer line or slightly farther, the fabric has the correct amount of stretch for the pattern (**A**).

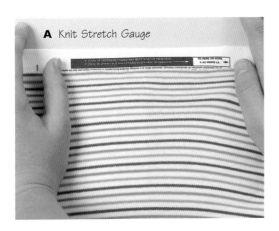

A Knit Stretch Gauge

TERMS TO KNOW

Bias—a diagonal line intersecting the lengthwise and crosswise grain on woven fabric. To "cut on the bias," cut diagonally across the fabric, at a 45° angle to the lengthwise grain. A pattern piece cut on the bias has more stretch and drape.

Fabric Width—the measurement of the fabric from selvage to selvage.

Fashion Fabric—the outer fabric of a garment.

Grain—either the lengthwise (running the length of the fabric) or crosswise (running the width of the fabric from selvage to selvage) thread in a woven fabric. Pieces are usually cut on the lengthwise grain so they drape appropriately. Crosswise threads have a little more stretch than lengthwise threads.

Interfacing—a type of fabric placed between the garment and the facing, adding body, strength and/or shape.

Layout—the guide for placing pattern pieces on the fabric for cutting.

Lining—the fabric layer on the inside of some garments, used to conceal construction seams—linings also make garments easier to slip on and off and reduce wrinkling.

Nap—fabrics with a nap reflect light differently depending upon which direction they're cut (examples include velvet and satin), or have a one-way pattern or design. If the fabric you choose has a nap, use the pattern layout labeled "with nap."

Nonwoven Fabric—a fabric that isn't woven or knit—nonwoven fabrics are manmade and bonded with adhesive.

One-Way Design—fabrics that have a printed or woven design that requires the pattern pieces be cut all in the same direction, using the "with nap" pattern layout, so the print isn't upside down on portions of the project.

Selvage—the firmly woven, finished edges on either side of yardage, running parallel to the lengthwise grain.

Warp—the threads running parallel to the selvage.

Weft—the threads running perpendicular to the selvage.

While you're shopping for your fabric, buy the interfacing and other notions and accessories you'll need to complete the project.

shopping for fabric

When you go to a fabric store, you'll notice that there are many different types of fabric, and they're usually organized according to these categories—fashion, home dec, quilting, etc. Fabric is available in different widths, such as 45″ and 60″, and is cut from a bolt, either folded or flat. For example, most 100% cotton quilting fabrics are 45″ wide and folded onto flat, rectangular bolts, while many home-dec fabrics are 60″ wide and rolled flat on tubes.

common-sense rules

Avoid forbidden fabrics. Read the pattern envelope and follow the advice for suggested fabrics. If it says "not suitable for napped fabrics and one-way designs," don't choose those fabrics. A skilled sewer might be able to make a pattern work in a forbidden fabric, but will spend extra time doing so.

Don't choose woven fabric for a "knits only" pattern—and vice versa. If it's a popular style, chances are similar patterns are available for woven fabrics—unless the style relies on a knit for its shape and appearance. A knit fabric won't work for traditional blue jeans and a swimsuit wouldn't be very practical in denim.

Buy fabrics you love and that look good next to your skin. If you don't love the fabric's texture, drape, color and appearance, don't buy it. If you don't love it before you cut, you probably won't wear the finished garment.

Follow your instincts. If you're questioning the suitability of a specific fabric for your chosen pattern, follow your instincts and don't buy it—or look for a different pattern that's suitable.

Start small with new fabrics. Try sewing a smaller project to get a feel for sewing a new fabric before tackling a large project. If you've never sewn on satin or velvet, making a wedding dress with a full train could lead to disaster.

Buy the best you can afford. Don't spend your valuable time sewing inferior fabric. Quality will make a difference in your sewing experience as well as the finished garment. This is an important rule for beginners. If the first things you sew aren't perfect, you'll still be happier wearing them if you use quality fabric that you love.

Pay attention to fabric widths. Make sure to buy yardage in the correct width for the size you're making. For some patterns, the only appropriate width is 54″ to 60″ because of the size or shape of the pattern pieces—look at the pattern guidesheet layout. Buying extra yardage may not work and piecing some of the garment sections may add unwanted seams in awkward places.

fabric preparation

preshrinking

For washable fabrics, simply wash and dry the yardage the same way you'll launder the finished garment. If the fabric comes out of the dryer wrinkled, press it before moving on to the next step.

For garments that will require dry cleaning, preshrink the yardage by taking it to the cleaners and asking them to steam-press it. To steam-press fabric at home, move a steam iron just above the fabric along the grainline, and allow the fabric to dry thoroughly before working with it.

getting it on grain

The most important thing to consider when cutting is the fabric grain. If you ignore the grain, the resulting garment might not fit correctly and could have an awkward drape.

1. Begin by tearing the fabric on the crossgrain near one cut edge. The tear should be done swiftly for best accuracy. Ask the fabric store clerk to tear the fabric instead of cutting it when purchasing the yardage. For fabrics that don't tear easily, pull a thread near the cut end; then cut across the fabric, cutting along the open space left behind as your cutting guide (**B**).

2. Check the fabric grain by laying the fabric flat and aligning a corner of it with the corner of your cutting table or another surface with a square corner—it should match up perfectly. If it's slightly off grain, fold the fabric in half lengthwise so the torn ends are even, and pin the layers together along the selvages. Wrinkles will form as you force the fabric on grain—press with a steam iron until the wrinkles disappear (**C**).

3. If the fabric is very off grain, pull and stretch it on the bias in the opposite direction of where it's coming up short (**D**); fold and steam the fabric as described above. If the fabric is washable, dampen it with warm water before pulling and stretching.

B Pull thread and cut on line to straighten end.

C Pin and steam-press wrinkles from fabric.

Selvages

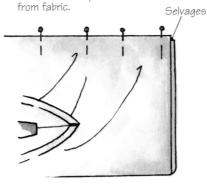

D Stretch fabric on bias to straighten grain.

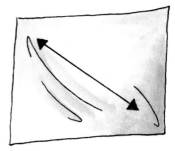

choosing a pattern

A PATTERN IS THE ROADMAP to a successful sewing project. Think of it as a blank canvas. It provides the framework of a garment—but you decide the fabric, color, skirt/shirt/pant length and trim. In short, you're the designer and can fashion a garment that reflects your personality and style.

book smart

When you go to the fabric store you'll see catalogs from major pattern companies, such as McCall's, Simplicity, Butterick, Vogue and Kwik Sew. The companies publish new catalogs each season to keep up with current fashion trends. In the back of the catalogs you'll find charts that help you determine the correct pattern size.

Patterns range in skill level from very simple to complicated. In general, the fewer number of pattern pieces, the easier the pattern. You'll find patterns for garments, accessories, home dec, crafts and more.

size wise

All major pattern companies follow a set of standard body measurements. These differ from ready-to-wear, so the size you choose for a pattern will be different (usually larger) than your ready-to-wear size.

The first step is to take your body measurements. Wear your usual undergarments. Use a tape measure that doesn't stretch, and take care not to hold the tape measure too tight or too loose. If possible, have a friend measure you. Stand in your usual posture—don't stand straight and suck in your stomach if you don't normally stand that way. Record your measurements and compare them to those on the pattern envelope.

Waistline—tie a string or piece of elastic around your waist to identify your natural waistline. Leave the string in place as a reference (**A**).

Hips—measure around the fullest part of the hip, which for women is generally 7″ to 9″ below the waist (**B**).

Bust—place the tape measure under your arms, straight across the back and across the fullest part of your bust (**C**).

Back Length—measure from the base of the neck down to the natural waist (marked with string). To find the starting point, bend your head forward and feel for the most prominent vertebra at the base of your neck (**D**).

ANATOMY OF A PATTERN ENVELOPE

You can learn a lot about a pattern just by looking at the envelope. Study the outside before delving into the mysteriously folded inner contents.

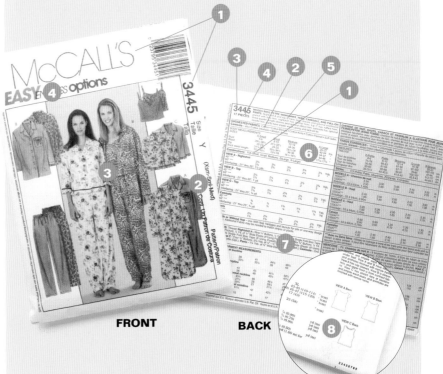

FRONT   BACK

FRONT: 1. Pattern Company and Style Number 2. Size 3. Photograph or Fashion Illustration 4. Labels

BACK: 1. Fabric Chart 2. Suggested Fabrics 3. Style Number 4. Number of Pattern Pieces 5. Garment Description 6. Body Measurement and Size Charts 7. Notions 8. Back Views

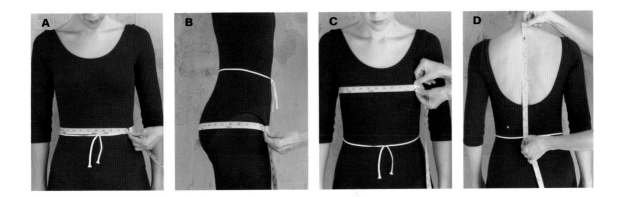

guidesheet

As you work your way through the pattern, the guidesheet will quickly become your best friend. It leads you step-by-step through the sewing process. Don't be afraid to mark the guidesheet—make notes, circle your size and layout diagrams.

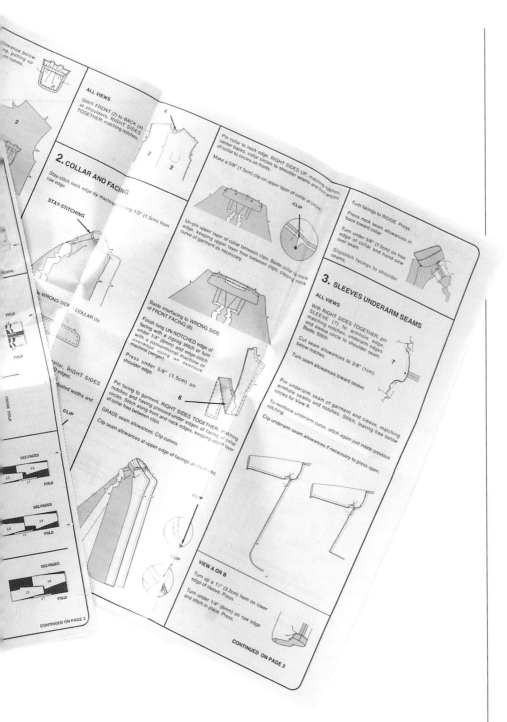

1. **Sewing Directions**— step-by-step instructions and illustrations show you how to make the project from start to finish. Read through these before starting your project.

2. **Fabric Key**—explains the illustrations: the fabric right side is usually shaded, the wrong side is white, interfacing is dotted and lining is cross-hatched.

3. **Illustrations**—shows the front and back of each view and includes style and construction details.

4. **General Information**— includes adjusting the pattern, cutting and marking, sewing, and a key to the symbols used on the pattern pieces.

5. **Cutting Layouts**—illustrates how to position the pattern pieces on the fabric to cut them out. A layout is shown for each view in every size and suggested fabric widths, as well as for fabric with or without nap.

6. **Pattern Pieces**—an illustration of each pattern piece is shown, with its name and number.

pattern pieces

Pattern pieces also contain a wealth of information. Once you understand what they mean, these seemingly meaningless dots, lines and triangles become helpful guides on your sewing journey.

1. Cutting Line—dark, solid line along the pattern outer edge—a scissors symbol is often shown on the line. Cut along this line. In some multisize patterns, each size has a different cutting line, such as a solid, dotted or dashed line.

2. Seamlines—the dashed line inside the cutting line indicates where you stitch. Multisize patterns (as shown) generally don't have the seamlines indicated.

3. Foldline—usually a bracket with arrows at each end and labeled "Place on Fold." Position the pattern piece with the foldline aligned on the fabric fold.

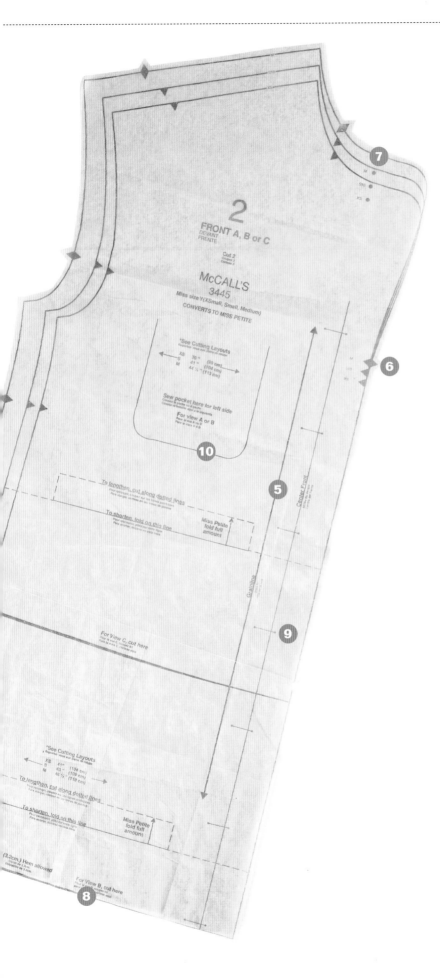

4. Adjustment Lines—two lines that mark where to lengthen or shorten the pattern before cutting out the fabric. If you need to alter the pattern, cut it on the double line; spread the pattern to lengthen, or overlap to shorten. Make sure the two lines remain parallel.

5. Grainline—straight line with arrows at each end. Position the pattern piece on the fabric with the grainline parallel to the fabric selvage or lengthwise grain.

6. Notches—single, double or triple diamonds printed on the cutting line. These are used to match fabric pieces when sewing.

7. Squares, Large and Small Dots, and Triangles—these additional marks indicate where to match fabric pieces, clip or start/stop stitching.

8. Hemline—shows the hem positioning and notes hem allowance. Turn up the hem at this line, adjusting as needed.

9. Button and Buttonhole Placement Marks—the buttonhole length is marked with solid lines. A button symbol or an "x" shows the button size and placement.

10. Detail Positions—solid or broken lines show placement of pockets and other details.

pattern layout

the pattern

1. Referring to the view you'd like to make, cut out the pattern pieces you'll be using. You needn't cut directly on the pattern line—½″ to 1″ margin around each piece is fine—but completely separate all pattern pieces for the project.

2. Press the pieces flat with a dry, warm iron. Pressing the pattern makes cutting easier and more accurate.

3. Organize the pattern pieces by separating those that will only be used for interfacing or lining, or will be cut in a contrasting fabric—then put them in numerical order.

layout

1. Circle the pattern layout guide you're using to avoid confusion. Carefully look over the layout before pinning the pattern pieces to the fabric.

2. Work on a large flat surface, such as a large table, to spread the fabric out flat. If the table isn't large enough, work with one section at a time. However, don't cut any pattern pieces until all the pieces are pinned in place. For best results, don't let fabric hang off the table edge—support it with a chair or roll it so it won't tug and stretch the area you're working on. If you must cut on the floor, a hard floor is better than carpet. If you must work on carpet, spread out a bedsheet or a

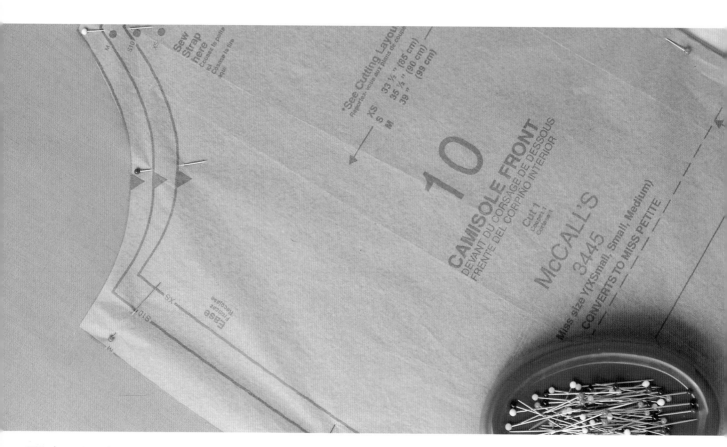

cardboard cutting surface and place the fabric on it—be diligent about keeping the fabric smooth and wrinkle-free.

3. Fold the fabric as noted in the layout, usually in half lengthwise—make sure the selvages are even.

4. Pin the pattern pieces in place. Pattern layouts use abbreviations and illustrations to show how to arrange the pieces and whether they should be placed with the printed side up or down. Each pattern company has its own abbreviations and illustration key, so read carefully.

5. Use a ruler or a measuring tape to make sure the pattern grainline is equidistant from the fabric edge for its entire length. Once in position, pin the pattern in place along the grainline; then double-check the grain, measuring the distance between the line and the fabric edge at each end (**A**).

6. When the grainline is straight, place pins around the pattern perimeter, ¼" inside the cutting line and perpendicular to the edge (**B**).

Space pins about 6" apart—or closer when working with slippery fabrics. If the pins will damage the fabric, pin only in the seam allowances.

7. If the fabric has a nap, like velvet, corduroy, stripes or a plaid, be sure to use the "with nap" layout, with all the pieces laid out in the same direction. If the envelope states the pattern isn't suitable for napped fabrics, don't be tempted to use them—the results will be disappointing.

8. If the fabric has a large design, you'll want to consider where the design will fall on the body when the garment is complete. For example, if your fabric has large roses on it, you probably don't want one of them to be centered at the bust point.

9. It's a good idea to take a break after you've pinned the project. Don't move the project. When you return, double-check your layout before cutting.

A Use a ruler or tape measure to ensure grainline is parallel to selvages.

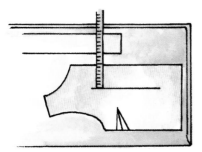

B Pin perpendicular to seamline.

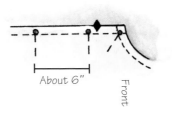

About 6"

Front

cutting

ACCURATELY CUTTING OUT A PATTERN is as easy as following the lines. But since cutting is permanent, double-check your layout to prevent mistakes.

To make cutting easier and more accurate, use fabric shears with long blades and a bent handle. These can be purchased for either left- or right-handed cutters. Keep them sharp and use them only for fabric (paper dulls scissors very quickly). Use long strokes for straight edges and shorter ones for curves.

If using a multisize pattern, double-check that you're cutting along the correct line. Trace over the line with a marker or pen if necessary (**A**).

You can use a rotary cutter and mat if you prefer (**B**). Make sure to keep the mat under the area being cut. Use a sharp blade and plastic ruler as a guide for the most accurate results. For greater accuracy, use shears for cutting curves or more difficult areas.

Don't use pinking shears to cut the fabric—pinking shears dull quickly and don't give an accurate edge to follow when sewing the seam.

Cut with the fabric grain for best results. The grain direction is usually indicated on the pattern cutting line by a small scissors illustration. If the fabric has a pile or nap, cut with the nap. Don't lift the fabric as you cut as this may cause inaccuracies. Instead, lay one hand flat on the pattern while cutting with the other hand.

Cut around notches or cut off the notch and make an ⅛" slash into the seam allowance at the notch point (**C**). Take care with the latter method—don't cut too deeply, and don't use this method for fabrics that ravel or rip easily.

Don't move the cut pieces or remove the pattern until all the necessary marks have been transferred to the fabric.

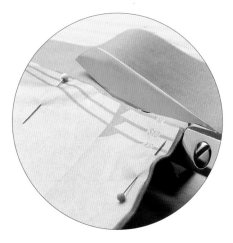

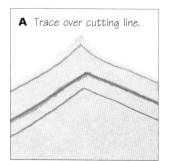

A Trace over cutting line.

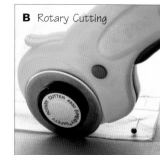

B Rotary Cutting

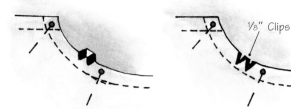

C Cut around notches ...

... or cut off and clip.

⅛" Clips

marking

marking

Transferring the pattern symbols to the fabric aids in construction. Use one of these methods to mark your fabric.

snips & clips

Snips and clips are good for marking notches and darts. Make shallow snips (⅛″ to ¼″ long) into the seam allowances. Don't cut all the way to the stitching line; this weakens the seam.

For single notches use one snip, for double notches use two, and so on (**A**). Notching (snipping V-shaped triangles out of the seam allowances) can be used to indicate centerlines, hemlines and foldlines as well as notches.

Check the seam allowance width. If the pattern has ¼″ seam allowances, snipping isn't an option; choose another marking method. Or cut around the notch (**B**).

fabric-marking pens

Use fabric-marking pens in combination with clipping and notching. For example, clip the dart legs at the seam allowance but draw the dart point with a marking pen (**C**). Non-permanent marking pens are also handy for marking embroidery or embellishment placement.

Air-soluble inks disappear with time. Water-soluble inks need to be washed away with water. Test markers beforehand; some are permanently set by heat. When purchasing markers, read the packaging carefully to see if they're temporary.

tracing paper

Choose the lightest color paper that's still visible on the fabric in case the marks don't come out. A serrated or sawtooth tracing wheel is most commonly used, but a smooth wheel is preferred for delicate fabrics. Work on a self-healing cutting mat or a piece of cardboard to avoid damaging the work surface.

Practice before using a tracing wheel for the first time; learn how much pressure to apply by tracing lines on fabric scraps. Place the paper colored side against the fabric wrong side, underneath the pattern tissue. Applying slight pressure, roll the tracing wheel along the lines using a ruler as a guide (**D**). Move the tracing paper after each mark to ensure coverage, and trace all of the nec-

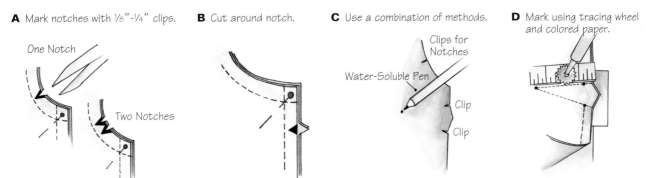

A Mark notches with ⅛″-¼″ clips.

One Notch

Two Notches

B Cut around notch.

C Use a combination of methods.

Clips for Notches

Water-Soluble Pen

Clip

Clip

D Mark using tracing wheel and colored paper.

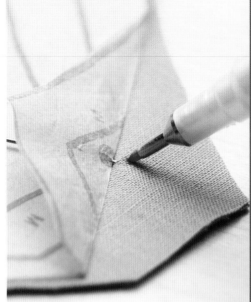

MARK WHAT?

Transfer markings for the following pattern details to ensure project success:

- Center front and center back
- Notches
- Dots and squares to be matched
- Darts
- Pleats
- Beginning and ending of gathered or eased areas
- Hemlines
- Placement lines for pockets, tabs, buttons, buttonholes, etc.
- Position lines for embroidery or decorative stitching

essary lines. Mark both fabric pieces at the same time whenever possible by placing folded tracing paper between the layers. Mark heavyweight fabrics individually.

If you want to trace stitching lines for a multisize pattern (stitching lines aren't marked on multisize patterns), first mark the stitching lines on the tissue, and then use the tissue as your guide.

Tracing paper isn't the best choice for marking on the fabric right side.

tailor's chalk

Tailor's chalk is a classic marking product and works on just about any fabric because it's easily removed and doesn't leave residue. Being easily removable may be a problem for projects that are handled a lot during construction. Tailor's chalk comes in a variety of colors and has a chalky or waxy consistency. It's available in a flat flake, a powder with an applicator or in pencil form. The chalk type works best on flat surfaces while the wax version performs better on textured fabrics, such as bouclé or corduroy.

straight pins

Use straight pins to mark details that will be immediately sewn or basted. They aren't a good long-term marking method since pins may slip out of the fabric with handling.

Use pins to indicate the ends of an opening, placement for a collar, or where to start and stop stitching.

Place pins perpendicular to each other to indicate a corner. Also use pins to mark the ends of buttonholes and the lower stop of a zipper.

Pin marking isn't recommended for fine fabrics or fabrics that retain pin holes. Use ball-point pins on knit fabrics.

pressure-sensitive stickers

Use stickers when ink, chalk or pins might damage the fabric. Some people find that using stickers is easier than marking, so they use them on all projects. Stickers are usually used to indicate interior pattern marks, such as pocket guidelines, snaps or buttons. Experiment with stickers found in office supply stores and draw placement markings on them.

interfacing

INTERFACING ADDS BODY AND CREATES STRUCTURE in garments. It stabilizes lighter-weight fabric and provides support behind buttons and buttonholes. There are three types of interfacing: knit, woven and nonwoven.

Knit—gives a softer, more draped effect.

Woven—adds stability and strength.

Nonwoven—adds strength; may also add stiffness.

Interfacing is available in both fusible and nonfusible types. Fusible interfacing is the easiest to work with; making it well suited for beginners.

Typically, the interfacing you use should be a slightly lighter weight than your fabric.

applying fusible interfacing

You should always follow the manufacturer's instructions when fusing interfacing, as there may be variations between different types of fusibles. However, these general guidelines usually apply:

1. Cut each pattern piece to be interfaced from fabric and interfacing.

2. Center the interfacing on the fabric, placing the rough (or shiny) side of the interfacing next to the fabric wrong side.

3. Cover the interfacing and fabric with a press cloth.

4. Place the iron on the interfacing, and press down firmly (with steam) for ten seconds, without sliding the iron back and forth. Move the iron to another position and repeat the process until the entire piece is fused.

5. Allow the fabric to cool and dry completely before moving it.

SOURCE | **Pellon Consumer Products,** pellonideas.com, (800) 223-5275, provided the interfacing.

seams

SEWING SEAMS ISN'T DIFFICULT. The pattern directions indicate how wide the seam allowances should be. Seams are the building block of any project, so stitch carefully to avoid puckers and ripples.

1. Place two pieces of fabric right sides together, aligning the cut edges and matching any notches.

2. Pin the edges together, placing the pins perpendicular to the edge and approximately 4″ apart.

3. With the pinned side on top, place the fabric under the presser foot. Line up the pinned fabric edge with the corresponding seam guideline on the sewing machine.

4. Lower the presser foot. Lower the needle into the fabric by turning the balance wheel.

5. Secure the stitches at the beginning and end of each seam by backstitching. Make two or three stitches, then stitch in reverse for two to three stitches. Stitch forward, stitching the remainder of the seam.

6. Stop stitching and remove pins as you encounter them. Sewing over pins can bend the pins, break the needle, and wear down the machine's feed dogs.

7. Take your time and make sure the fabric edges stay even with the seam guideline on themachine. The easiest way to mess up a seam is to sew too quickly. Watch the fabric edge, not the needle.

8. Backstitch at the end of the seam.

9. Raise the needle by turning the wheel. Raise the presser foot. Pull the fabric out from under the foot toward the back of the machine. Trim the threads close to the fabric.

seam finishes

Every seam needs a good finish. Some finishes are more appropriate for one fabric than for another, so test different seam finishes on a scrap of the project fabric. The seam finish prevents raveling and helps the seam withstand wear and cleaning. A good seam finish is smooth and doesn't add much bulk to the seam or show on the project right side.

Pinked Finish: Use pinking shears to trim along the edge of firmly woven fabrics. Or stitch ¼″ from the edge and then pink.

Machine Zigzag Finish: This is good for all fabric weights. Stitch close to the fabric edge.

Overcast Finish: This treatment is suitable for all knit and woven fabrics. Use the overcast stitch on a conventional machine or a serger 3-thread overlock so the stitch overlaps the fabric edge.

pivoting

Sewing straight seams is easy. However, there "will be times when you need to turn a corner. Pivot at corners using the following technique.

1. Stitch to the corner; stop with the needle down in the fabric. Lift the presser foot.

2. Turn the fabric and line up the edge with the stitching guideline.

3. Lower the presser foot; continue stitching.

Machine Zigzag

Pinked

Overcast

pressing

ALTHOUGH SOME PEOPLE USE the terms pressing and ironing interchangeably, pressing is an up-and-down motion that shapes with pressure. Ironing is a back-and-forth motion for removing wrinkles. If you use the right tools and learn the proper techniques, pressing can transform a garment from looking homemade to looking professional.

pressing matters to consider

1. Test first to determine how heat and steam will affect the fabric.

2. Press as you sew—don't wait until you finish the project. Never cross a seam, pleat, dart or tuck with stitching until it's been pressed.

3. Press on the fabric wrong side.

4. Use a press cloth, if necessary, to protect the fabric, especially when pressing from the right side.

5. Press lightly at first to prevent seam allowances from imprinting on the project right side.

6. Allow the fabric to cool (and dry, if using steam) before moving it.

7. Never press over pins or basting. This can leave imprints or dimples that are very difficult to remove. Pressing over pins can also scratch the iron's soleplate or melt plastic pinheads.

pressing area

Set up a pressing area near your sewing machine at a comfortable height. For pressing while standing, ergonomic experts suggest setting the ironing surface about 8″ below the elbow.

For pressing while sitting, place the board at the same height as your sewing table, at a right angle to the sewing machine. An ironing board with adjustable height lets you customize its position whether you're sitting or standing. You'll be more apt to use your pressing tools if they're within easy reach.

SOURCE | **Nancy's Notions,** nancysnotions.com, (800) 833-0690, provided the iron.

elastic casing waistband

AN ELASTIC WAISTBAND IS EASY to make and comfortable to wear—so it's perfect for pajama pants, lounge pants or casual skirts. The most basic elastic waistband is made by folding down an extension of the garment fabric to form a casing and inserting the elastic.

If your pattern doesn't have an elastic waistband, add 4" above the waistline.

1. Baste the seam allowances open about 4" below the upper edge to keep them flat. This makes it easier to insert the elastic (**A**).

2. Zigzag- or serge-finish the garment upper edge. Turn down the casing the amount specified in the pattern (usually 2¼") and press the fold. Stitch close to the fold, beginning and ending at a side seam, overlapping the stitching.

3. Stitch along the lower edge of the casing, leaving a 2" opening at one side seam (**B**).

4. Measure your waist and subtract 5" to allow for stretch and a snug fit. Be sure this length can stretch around the widest part of your hips; if not, increase the length. Measure the elastic to this length and test it by wrapping it around your waist while you're sitting down, trying different amounts of stretch until you're satisfied with the fit. Cut the elastic this length.

5. Attach a safety pin or bodkin to one end of the elastic, and insert it into the casing opening. Pin the opposite end of the elastic to the garment to prevent it from getting lost in the casing. Guide the elastic through the casing. Remove the pin and overlap the elastic ends, making sure the elastic isn't twisted in the casing. Zigzag securely, stitching through both elastic layers (**C**). Remove the basting.

6. Machine stitch the casing opening closed. Distribute the casing fabric fullness evenly around the elastic; pin at side and center-back seams. Topstitch along the seams to prevent the elastic from rolling and shifting (**D**).

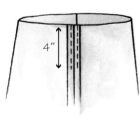

A Baste seam allowances.

4"

B Stitch lower edge of casing.

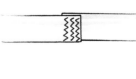

C Stitch elastic ends.

D Stitch in the ditch at seamlines.

hems

THERE ARE MANY WAYS TO STITCH HEMS—some hems are sewn by hand and others by machine. When choosing a method, consider the fabric, the garment style and your personal preference.

Finish the raw edge of the hem allowance before stitching the hem in place. To learn about several options for finishing raw edges, see "Seam Finishes" on page 162.

hand-hemming stitches

These stitches are worked either flat or "blind." Flat stitches are visible on the garment wrong side, going over the hem cut edge and into the garment. Blind stitches are hidden between the hem allowance and the garment.

1. Turn up the hem allowance along the hemline and press the fold. Pin the hem in place through both layers. Pin ¼″ below and parallel to the edge.

2. Thread a hand-sewing needle with no more than 18″ of thread. Knot one end and stitch with a single thread. Select one of the following hand stitches to secure the edge. Work on a flat surface, and don't pull the stitches too tight or the hem will ripple.

When stitching into the garment, take the smallest stitch possible, picking up only one or two threads. This will keep the stitches nearly invisible on the garment right side. Secure the first and last stitches with a backstitch. (For left-handed stitchers, work in the opposite direction described.)

Slant Hemming Stitch. This is the least durable hem because so much thread is exposed. Working from right to left, secure the thread on the wrong side of the hem, and then bring it up through the hem edge. Take a stitch into the garment ¼″ to ⅜″ from the first stitch, then insert the needle into the hem edge the same distance away (**A**).

Slipstitch. For a folded or bound hem edge, select this stitch. Working from right to left, bring the first stitch out through the fold of the hem or hem binding, take a small stitch into the garment, and slip the needle into the fold about ¼″ (**B**).

> When hand sewing, cut the thread lengths 18″ or shorter—any longer and the thread knots and frays easily, causing frustration.

A Work slant hemming stitch from right to left.

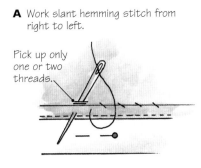

Pick up only one or two threads.

B Work slipstitch right to left picking up ¼″ of finished hem edge.

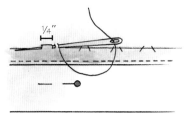

¼″

Catchstitch. Choose this stitch for hemming knits and stretch fabrics. Working from left to right, fasten the thread on the wrong side of the hem. Take a stitch in the garment fabric, then take the next stitch into the hem approximately ¼" to ⅜" away, making sure the thread crosses over itself to create an X (**C**).

A blind catchstitch is worked similarly, but within the hem, pulling the hem edge back to work the stitches (**D**).

Blind-Hem Stitch. This is the most versatile stitch, and it works well with most hem finishes and fabrics. Working from right to left, fold back the hem edge, and fasten the thread to it. Take a stitch in the garment fabric, then take the next stitch into the hem, approximately ¼" away (**E**).

machine-stitched hems

Whether you're looking for an invisible hem or a more decorative one, your sewing machine is faster than hand stitching.

Blind Hem. Done correctly, this stitch is sturdy and inconspicuous. It can be used on many fabrics and is especially suitable for full skirts and children's clothing. It works best on straight rather than curved hem edges. The stitch consists of three to six straight stitches stitched into the hem allowance, followed by a zigzag that barely bites into the garment fabric. Set your machine for a blind-hem stitch, and attach the blind-hem foot (consult your machine manual for specifics).

With the wrong side of the garment face up, fold the hem allowance under, leaving the upper ¼" of the hem edge exposed. Place the garment fold to the left of the foot and the hem edge to the right. Stitch along the hem allowance so the zigzag just barely bites into the fold (**F**). If the stitches bite into the fold too much, reduce the stitch width.

Topstitched Hem. If you're looking for a sporty or casual look, consider a topstitched hem. The hem stitches are visible on the garment right side and can be anything from a single row of straight stitching to several rows of decorative stitching.

For woven fabrics, turn up the hem allowance the desired amount, and finish the hem edge by folding it under ½". Hand baste the hem in place along the inner fold. From the garment right

---

C Work catchstitch from left to right.

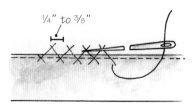

D Work blind catchstitch between hem allowance and garment.

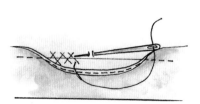

E Work blind-hem stitch from right to left.

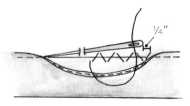

CATCHSTITCH
(hand-hemmed)

TOPSTITCH
(machine-hemmed)

side, topstitch just below the basting. Keep the stitching straight and parallel to the hemline (**G**). Remove the basting.

For knits, especially lightweight ones, use a narrow topstitched hem. Trim the hem allowance to ⅝″ and press it up along the hemline. Hand baste ½″ from the raw edge. From the garment right side, stitch ½″ and then ⅜″ from the hem

line fold or use a twin needle to stitch both rows at once (**H**). Remove the basting.

Narrow Hem. When the hem is narrow and the stitching doesn't need to be hidden, choose this hem treatment. Trim the hem allowance to ½″. Press under the edge ¼″, then press it under ¼″ again. Stitch along the inner fold (**I**).

F Zigzag just catches fold.

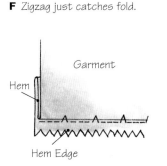

Garment

Hem

Hem Edge

G Baste hem edge from wrong side; topstitch on right side after basting.

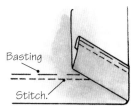

Basting

Stitch.

H Turn up hem and baste; double topstitch in place.

Basting

⅝″

I Turn up ¼″ twice and topstitch.

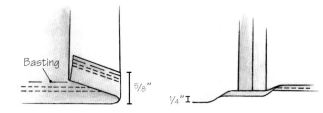

¼″ **I**

zippers

ONE OF THE MOST SATISFYING sewing techniques to master is inserting a zipper quickly and easily with professional-looking results. Whether you choose a centered, lapped or invisible application, practicing the following methods will calm your fears about making a project that requires a zipper.

centered zipper

The most common zipper opening is centered down the front or back of a garment. Also, zippers placed in purses, pillows and other items usually use a centered application. Centered zippers are ideal for everyday clothes, especially for fabric that's heavyweight, has thick pile or needs to be matched at the seam.

In a centered closure, the zipper is concealed by two flaps of fabric running along either side. When completed, two lines of stitching (one on each side of the zipper) are visible from the right side.

1. Placement for the lower zipper stop is usually marked on the pattern. Stitch the seam with a normal stitch length below this mark, backstitching at the mark. Above the mark, machine-baste the seam. Press the entire seam open.

2. With the garment wrong side up, place the closed zipper right side down on the seam allowances with the zipper teeth centered along the basted seamline and the lower stop just below the end of the basting. (Placing the zipper lower stop below the basting ensures you won't stitch over the metal stop while topstitching the zipper lower end.) Pin the zipper in place through the seam allowances only; don't pin through to the outside of the garment (**A**).

3. Using a zipper foot, baste the zipper to the seam allowances only (**B**).

INVISIBLE

REGULAR

4. For best topstitching results, use a stitch slightly longer than regular sewing, but not as long as a basting stitch. Be careful to stitch an even distance from the teeth. If this is difficult, use a topstitching guide, or center ½″-wide cellophane tape along the seam and stitch just beyond the tape edges.

5. From the garment right side, topstitch the zipper in place using a zipper foot. To prevent ripples, sew both sides of the zipper in the same direction. Begin at the zipper upper edge and stitch to the end of the basted seamline, then pivot and stitch over to the seamline. Don't backstitch; instead, leave a thread tail to pull to the wrong side. Repeat to sew the zipper opposite side (**C**).

6. Use a hand-sewing needle to pull the thread ends to the wrong side and tie off. Remove the basting and press with a cool iron.

lapped zipper

When zippers first became popular, most were sewn with a lapped closure. Lapping a zipper hides the teeth better, which is why it's often the application of choice for dressy clothing or when the zipper color doesn't match the fabric exactly. It's also an excellent choice for delicate fabric or pile fabrics that can catch in the zipper teeth.

A lapped zipper is concealed by a fabric flap; only one stitching line is visible from the right side. Lapped zippers are often used in the left side seams of pants and skirts.

1. For a lapped zipper, the seam allowances should be at least ⅝″ wide. Stitch the garment seam below the lower stop with a normal stitch length, and machine-baste the seam above the lower zipper stop. Press the seam open.

A Pin zipper in place through seam allowances only.
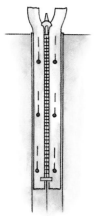

B Baste zipper to seam allowances.
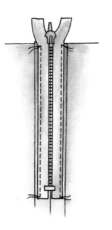

C Topstitch zipper.
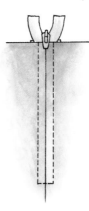

2. With the garment wrong side up, place the closed zipper right side down on the seam allowances with the lower stop just below the end of the basting. Align the left edge of the zipper tape with the raw edge of the left seam allowance and pin in place through the seam allowance only. Using a zipper foot and a ¼″ seam allowance, stitch the zipper tape to the seam allowance only (**D**).

3. Flip the zipper to the left so it's face up. This will create a fold in the seam allowance—but not in the zipper tape. Bring this fold close to (but not touching) the zipper coils. Sew the zipper in place close to the edge of the fold (**E**).

4. From the garment right side, topstitch the left-hand side of the zipper (the overlap) starting at the lower end and leaving long thread tails. Slowly stitch across the zipper, then up the left side ⅜″ from the seamline (**F**).

5. Pull the thread ends to the wrong side and tie off. Remove the basting and press with a cool iron.

invisible or hidden zipper

Invisible zippers make the zipper application look like a seam, and are often substituted for conventional zippers. Unlike a centered or lapped zipper, an invisible zipper is inserted into a fully open seam.

1. When inserting an invisible zipper, it's helpful to use a foot with a groove on the underside that makes the zipper coil stand away from the tape while stitching (invisible zipper foot or pintuck foot). However, you can also use a regular presser foot or zipper foot. A zipper foot is required for the final application step. Using a regular presser foot over the zipper coil may keep the foot from being lowered completely—preventing the tension

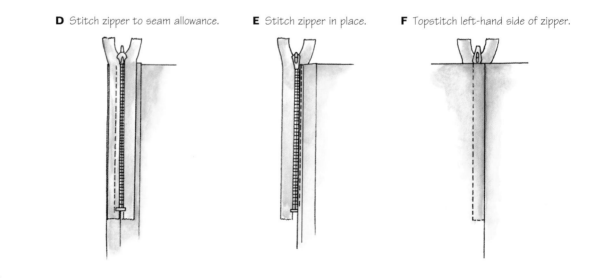

D Stitch zipper to seam allowance. **E** Stitch zipper in place. **F** Topstitch left-hand side of zipper.

discs from being engaged on some machines, causing looped or skipped stitches. In that case, use a zipper foot (either conventional or invisible).

2. Mark the stitching lines on each garment piece by pressing under the seam allowances or basting along the seamline where the zipper will be inserted. Open the zipper and press it flat from the wrong side so the coil stands away from the tape.

3. Place the zipper face down on the fabric right side, with the coil along the seamline and the zipper tape in the seam allowance. Pin in place and hand baste if desired. Using a regular presser foot, lower the needle right next to the top of the zipper coil. As you lower the presser foot, flatten the coil with a seam ripper or large needle. As you begin to sew, the coil will automatically unfold. Stitch next to the coil but not on top of it, as this will keep the zipper from opening and closing.

Stitch from the upper to the lower edge (**G**).

4. Repeat to sew the other zipper side to the remaining garment piece right side. Close the zipper.

5. To finish the seam below the zipper, use a conventional zipper foot, and pin the garment right sides together along the seamline. Lower the needle into the seam exactly where the zipper stitching stops. Without backstitching, begin sewing (you may need to use the hand wheel), while pulling the zipper away from the seam to keep it clear (**H**). Sew the seam, pull the thread ends through to one side of the seam and tie. The result should be a smooth seam with no puckers where the zipper ends.

G Coil opens up when flattened by presser foot.

H Begin stitching seam just at zipper end.

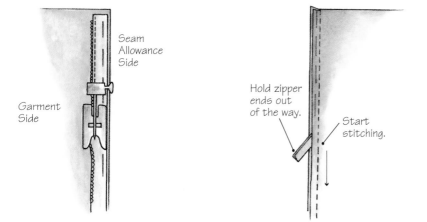

Seam Allowance Side

Garment Side

Hold zipper ends out of the way.

Start stitching.

buttons & buttonholes

A BUTTON AND BUTTONHOLE can be used to close any type of overlapped edge. Buttons are a good choice for any area that will experience pulling or straining, such as garment center fronts and backs, waistbands or tab-top curtains. In addition to their functional aspects, buttons and buttonholes can also be used for decorative purposes.

Patterns recommend a button size and buttonhole length. If you're using a button size other than the one recommended on the pattern envelope, adjust the buttonhole length. You may also need to adjust the pattern to accommodate a larger button so the buttons don't hang off the garment edge or look too big for the project.

To determine the proper buttonhole length, measure the button's diameter and depth. Add these two measurements together and add ⅛" to allow for the finished buttonhole ends (**A**). For ball and odd-shaped buttons, cut a ¼"-wide paper strip and wrap it around the button. Pinch-mark where the strip meets at the button edge. Holding the strip ends together, slide the paper off the button and flatten the loop. Measure the strip from the fold to the mark and add ⅛" to determine the buttonhole length (**B**).

making a buttonhole

Machine-stitched buttonholes are the easiest to make and can be successfully executed on most fabrics. Most machines have a built-in stitch or special attachment for stitching buttonholes, but any machine with an adjustable-width zigzag stitch can perform the task. Make the buttonholes before attaching the buttons. For most projects, making the buttonholes and sewing on the buttons are the final steps.

1. Make a sample buttonhole on a scrap of the project fabric. Use the same interfacing, thread and same number of fabric layers that the actual buttonhole will be sewn through. Use this test buttonhole to make sure the button will pass easily, but not sloppily, through the buttonhole.

2. Refer to the pattern to mark the buttonhole placement on the fabric right side. For clothing, try on the garment and be sure the button and

A Diameter + Depth + ⅛" = Buttonhole Length

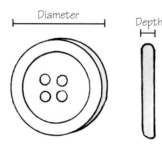

B Wrap strip around button and mark. Measure from fold to mark.

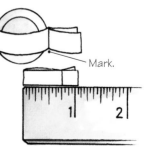

buttonhole placements are in the desired locations; adjust them if necessary.

3. If the buttonhole area hasn't been interfaced, cut lightweight fusible interfacing rectangles about 1″ wider and longer than the buttonhole. Center and fuse an interfacing rectangle to the fabric wrong side at each buttonhole. Position the interfacing so the least amount of stretch is parallel to the buttonhole.

4. Follow the instructions in your machine manual to stitch the buttonhole, following the placement markings. Start and stop stitching at the buttonhole end that's nearest the project finished edge.

5. Pull the threads to the wrong side and knot the ends. Apply seam sealant to the knot and buttonhole center. Allow to dry. Or secure the stitches by taking three or four small stitches along one buttonhole side.

6. Insert a straight pin across both ends of each buttonhole. Insert the point of small scissors or a seam ripper into the buttonhole center and cut toward each end (**C**). The pins prevent you from

accidentally cutting through the bar tacks and fabric at either end of the buttonhole. Or use a buttonhole cutter and block to cut open the buttonhole.

sewing on a button

Knowing how to sew on a button will keep you from paying, and waiting, for someone else to do it.

There are two basic types of buttons: sew-through and shank. Sew-through buttons have two or four holes drilled through them and can be sewn on by hand or machine. If you're sewing on just one button, it's just as fast to sew it on by hand. But if you have multiple buttons to attach, use the machine to speed up the task.

Sew-through buttons used for decorative purposes can be sewn flat against the fabric, but functional sew-through buttons, used in conjunction with a buttonhole, should be attached with a thread shank. The shank leaves room for the overlap's fabric layers to fit under the button without pulling or distorting the fabric. Shank buttons have a metal or plastic loop that takes the place of a thread shank. These buttons must be attached by hand.

C Beginning at center, cut to each end.

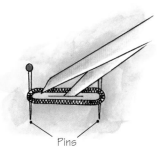

Pins

When hand sewing, cut the thread length 18″ or shorter—any longer and the thread will knot and fray too easily.

button placement

1. Stitch and cut open the buttonhole(s).

2. Lay the buttonhole over the corresponding underlap, aligning the appropriate pattern markings. For example, for a button-front blouse, align the center-front markings.

3. For horizontal buttonholes, insert a straight pin through the buttonhole ⅛″ from the bar tack closest to the finished edge. Lift the overlap and mark the point where the pin entered the underlap. For vertical buttonholes, insert the pin ⅛″ from the upper bar tack (**D**).

4. Place two-hole and shank buttons so the shank or holes are parallel to the buttonhole.

hand-stitched sew-through buttons

1. Mark the button position on the project right side as described in "Button Placement."

2. Cut approximately 18″ of thread, and run it through beeswax to help strengthen it and prevent tangles. Thread the needle. Knot the ends together to create a double strand.

3. Take a small backstitch at the marked button position on the fabric right side. Trim the thread tails close to the knot (**E**).

4. Working from the the button back to the front, insert the needle through one hole. Center the button over the marked position. Insert the needle through another hole in the button and then through the fabric.

5. Slip a toothpick or sewing-machine needle between the thread and button (**F**). Take three or four stitches through each pair of holes, ending with the needle and thread on the project wrong side.

6. Bring the needle and thread to the right side under the button. Remove the toothpick or needle. Gently pull up the button so the slack thread is between the button and the fabric. Wrap the threads under the button several times with the needle thread to form a shank. Insert the needle through the loop to create a knot (**G**). For extra security, insert the needle and thread through the shank and clip the threads close to the shank. Dot the thread ends with seam sealant. Or take a small stitch into the fabric, tie a knot, and clip the thread close to the knot.

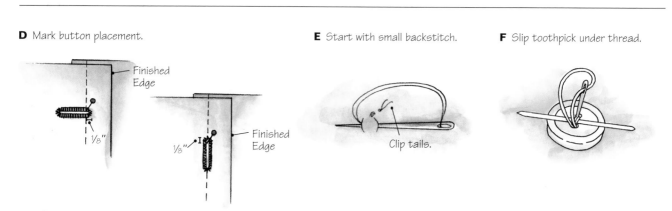

D Mark button placement.

Finished Edge

⅛″

Finished Edge

⅛″

E Start with small backstitch.

Clip tails.

F Slip toothpick under thread.

machine-stitched sew-through buttons

1. Mark the button position on the project right side as described in "Button Placement."

2. Using a glue stick, dab glue on the button back. Center and press it in place. Let the glue dry.

3. If your sewing machine has a button-sewing stitch, select it. If it doesn't, set the stitch length to "0" and lower the feed dogs.

4. Attach the button foot. Adjust the stitch width to span the button's holes. If the presser foot doesn't have an adjustable shank guide, insert a machine needle into the groove on the button foot. Use the hand wheel to check that the needle swings the correct distance between the holes (**H**).

5. Take several stitches to secure the button. Lock the stitches by turning the width to "0" and sewing several stitches in the same button hole.

6. Lift the presser foot, and remove the needle under the stitches. Without cutting the thread, move to the next button position and repeat.

7. When all of the buttons are sewn on, cut the threads halfway between the buttons. Thread the ends through the buttons' holes. Wrap them around the slack threads (between the button and the fabric) to form a shank. Tie a knot (**I**), and clip the ends close to the shank. Dot the knot with seam sealant.

shank buttons

1. Mark the button position on the project right side as described in "Button Placement." Refer to "Hand-Stitched Sew-Through Buttons" to prepare the needle and thread. Take a stitch at the placement mark.

2. Center the button shank over the placement mark so the shank is parallel to the buttonhole. Insert the needle through the shank and into the fabric three to four times, ending with the needle on the fabric right side (**J**).

3. Take several small stitches under the button or knot the thread ends to secure the stitches. Dot the knot with seam sealant.

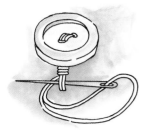

G Wrap threads to form shank; insert needle through loops to tie off.

H Use button-stitching foot to sew on buttons with zigzag stitch.

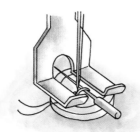

I Wrap threads around shank and tie off.

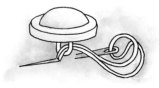

J Sew on a shank button.

closures

ON PAGES 172 TO 175, YOU LEARNED ABOUT BUTTONS, but there are other closure options to choose from. When it comes to finishing a garment or decorative project, choosing the right closure can make the difference between a professional or handmade look. With the array of fasteners on the market, choosing the one that works best for your project and knowing how to apply it is a snap.

snaps

These sturdy closures are often used on children's clothing, men's shirts, outerwear and at cuff openings. There are three basic types of snaps: sew-on, covered and no-sew.

Sew-on snaps have two basic components: a ball insertion piece (male) and a socket, or receiving, piece (female).

Covered snaps are just that, sew-on snaps that have been covered with fabric to coordinate with a project. They come pre-covered in neutral colors, or you can cover them as you would a button (see "Covering a Button" on page 181).

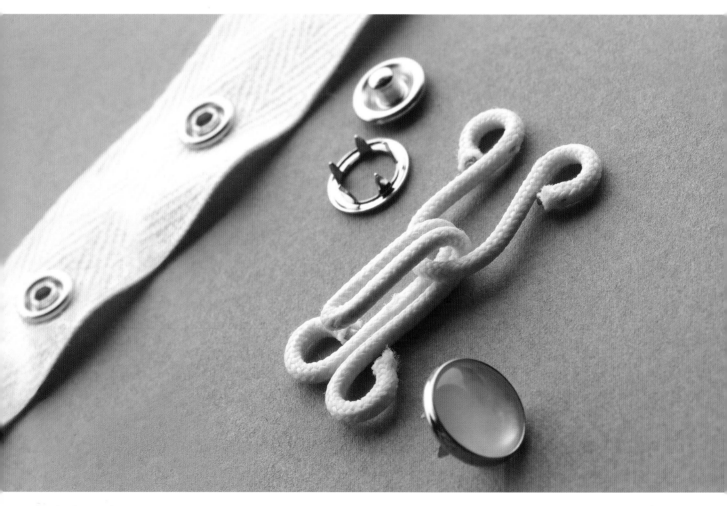

to attach covered and sew-on snaps:

1. Finish the area where the snap will be inserted.

2. Carefully measure each snap's placement, marking where the center of the snap will be positioned with an air- or water-soluble marker. Secure the socket snap pieces to the right side of the underlap and the ball pieces on the underside of the overlap.

3. Working from the back side of the mark, push a pin through the fabric at the mark and then through the snap piece (**A**). Position the snap piece against the fabric; remove the pin. Using coordinating thread, take a few hand stitches through each opening around the snap edge to secure it.

4. Repeat until each snap component is secured. On the overlap, catch only the lower fabric layer to prevent the stitching from showing on the garment right side.

to insert a no-sew snap:

No-sew snaps have four components: the ball and socket pieces and two additional rings with prongs that hold both the ball and socket pieces in place (**B**).

1. Finish the area where the snap will be inserted. The snap needs to be inserted through at least two fabric layers or one layer of thick or interfaced fabric for stability.

2. On the fabric overlap wrong side, use a fabric-marking pen to mark each snap's position.

3. Place a prong piece point side up on a padded surface. Push a pin from the fabric wrong side to the right side at the mark. Align the prong ring center with the pin. Push the fabric firmly onto the prongs until the fabric touches the ring base (**C**), and remove the pin.

4. Place the back side of the socket piece with the raised center over the prongs. Center a hard

---

A Position sew-on snaps with a pin.   **B** No-Sew Snaps   **C** Insert prong piece from fabric wrong side.

plastic thread spool over the socket and tap it with a hammer or rubber mallet until the prongs are secured in the socket piece (**D**).

5. On the fabric underlap right side, precisely measure and mark where the center of the receiving snap portions will be located. Push a pin to the fabric wrong side at the mark.

6. Align the prong piece center with the pin and push the prongs through from the wrong side to the right side. Center the receiving piece over the prongs and use the same spool and hammer method to secure the prongs. Repeat until all the snaps are inserted.

snap tape

If sewing or inserting snaps is too daunting or time-consuming for your taste, use snap tape instead. Using snap tape is faster because you don't have to mark and install each snap.

Snap tape consists of a ¾″-wide cotton band that has pre-inserted snaps, commonly placed 1½″ apart. Stitch along the tape lengthwise edges to secure it to the fabric. Use a zipper foot to avoid hitting snaps as you sew. For added security and stability, stitch across the tape width ¼″ on either side of each snap (**E**).

hook & eyes

Hook-and-eye closures work well to fasten edges that meet or overlap. They're usually applied at a single point, but they can be used to close an entire opening.

There are two basic types of hook-and-eye closures: general purpose and special purpose General-purpose hooks and eyes can be used for edges that meet or overlap. They range in size from fine (size 0) to heavy (size 3) and are available in nickel or black finishes and some colors. The general-purpose hook shape is available with either a straight or a round eye. Straight eyes are used on lapped edges; round eyes are used for edges that meet or abut.

D Place a spool over the snap and hit with a hammer.

E Stitch across snap tape for extra security.

Special-purpose hooks and eyes are usually heavier and larger than general-purpose hooks and eyes. Covered hooks and eyes used on fur garments and jackets fall into this category, as well as the flat hook-and-eye sets made specifically for waistband closures.

edges that meet

1. Use a hook and round eye, and sew both parts to the project wrong side through only one fabric layer. No stitches should be visible on the project right side.

2. Position the hook about $\frac{1}{16}''$ in from the garment edge. Whipstitch around each circular end section, and then slide the needle through the fabric layers and come up at the hook end. Take three or four stitches across the bend of the hook to hold it flat against the fabric. Secure the threads.

3. Position the eye on the opposite side of the opening so the loop extends about $\frac{1}{8}''$ from the finished edge. The garment edges should meet when the hook and eye are joined. Stitch around each loop end and across the bars, and then secure the threads (**F**).

edges that overlap

1. Use a hook and straight eye. Position the hook on the overlap wrong side so the hook end is about $\frac{1}{8}''$ from the edge. Whipstitch around the circular end, and then slide the needle through the fabric layers and surface at the hook end. Take three or four stitches across the bend of the hook to hold it flat. Secure the threads. The stitches should not be visible on the garment right side.

2. Overlap the edges. Push a pin through the fabric layers at the end of the hook. Mark the right side of the underlap where the pin enters the fabric.

3. Center the eye vertically on the marked spot. Whipstitch around each end; secure the threads (**G**).

F Stitch hook and eye to secure.

G Attach a hook to wrong side of overlap. Attach eye to right side of overlap.

hook-and-eye tape

For faster hook-and-eye application, use hook-and-eye tape. It functions the same way as snap tape, only with a centered opening instead of lapped edges. For extra stability stitch around each hook and loop as shown (**H**).

Stitch the tape to the folded-under layer or facing to prevent the stitching from showing on the project right side.

hook-and-loop tape

Hook-and-loop tape can be used for almost any closure. It can also be substituted for snaps, hooks and eyes, and buttons. This versatile closure has a soft-looped receiving side and a bristly-hook fastening side. The tape comes in various colors and widths, but is usually ¾″ wide. It's sold by the inch and as shorter strips, squares or dots.

Although hook-and-loop tape can be either sew-in or self-adhesive, sew-in is recommended as it provides greater stability and won't peel away from fabric with wear.

to attach hook-and-loop tape

1. Finish the seam or edges where the hook-and-loop tape will be used. The edges should overlap at least ½″ more than the tape width.

2. On the underlap, measure ¼″ from the upper edge to ¼″ from the lower edge. Cut a length of hook-and-loop tape that measurement.

3. On the underlap right side, align the looped portion ¼″ from the upper edge and ¼″ in from the long opening edge; pin in place.

4. Match the bobbin thread to the garment fabric. With the hook-and-loop tape side up, secure by edgestitching all four sides (**I**).

5. Repeat this method to apply the hook side to the overlap wrong side. Secure the hook-and-loop tape to close.

6. To attach hook-and-loop squares or dots, carefully measure and mark the placement of both the hook and loop portions. Center the square or dot on the mark (the loop piece on the underlap right side, the hook piece on the underside of the overlap).

H Stitch around each hook and loop.

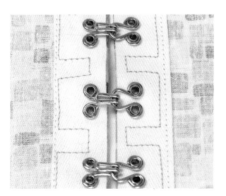

I Secure hook-and-loop tape.

covering a button

A covered button makes for a clean, polished look that coordinates with the project. Use a conventional button-covering kit, or cover your own button with these simple techniques.

To cover a button using a kit:

A button kit includes the following pieces: holder, button shell, button back, and a metal or plastic pusher (**1**). The button shell and back can be either metal or nylon and come in a variety of sizes.

1. Cut a fabric circle twice the diameter of the button. Center the fabric right side down on the indented side of the holder.

2. Gently center the convex side of the button shell on the fabric and press it into the holder. Tuck the extra fabric inside the shell's back.

3. Place a button back shank side up over the tucked-in fabric, making sure all raw fabric edges are concealed. Use the pusher to snap the back securely into the shell.

To cover a standard button without using a kit:

1. Cut a fabric circle twice the diameter of the button. With a needle and a single thread, sew tiny running stitches along the fabric edge (**2**).

2. Center the button on the fabric and pull the thread ends to gather the raw edges, encasing the button.

3. Sew several stitches through the gathered fabric as close as possible to the button. Secure the thread end, and trim the excess fabric.

To cover a snap:

1. Cut a fabric circle three to four times larger than the snap's diameter.

2. Using an awl or a thick needle, punch a small hole in the circle center.

3. Sew small running stitches around the fabric edge. Place the snap right side down on the fabric wrong side, aligning the circle hole with the snap's ball or socket. Gather the fabric to the back as for the button. Secure the fabric and cut off the excess (**3**).

4. Repeat with the opposite snap component.

(See "Buttons & Buttonholes" on page 172 for information on sewing on buttons and making buttonholes.)

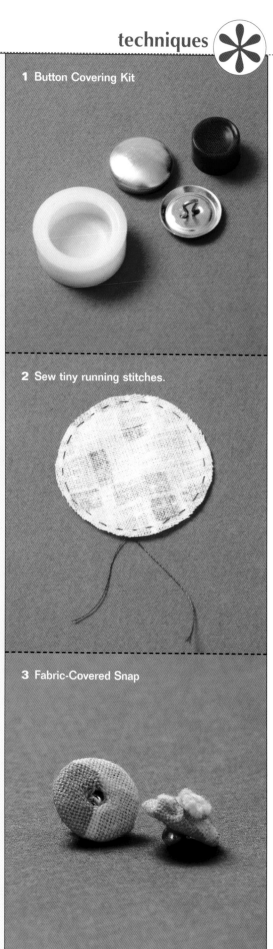

1 Button Covering Kit

2 Sew tiny running stitches.

3 Fabric-Covered Snap

gathering

IN JUST A FEW EASY STEPS, you can transform a flat piece of fabric into one with shape, movement and grace. Gathering is often seen on garments at the waistline, cuffs, yoke, sleeves or as ruffles. It's also used in home-dec projects, such as bedskirts and window treatments. Gathering allows you to fit a long piece of fabric (such as a skirt) onto a shorter piece of fabric (such as a waistband). The result is soft, evenly spaced folds that add shape to the project.

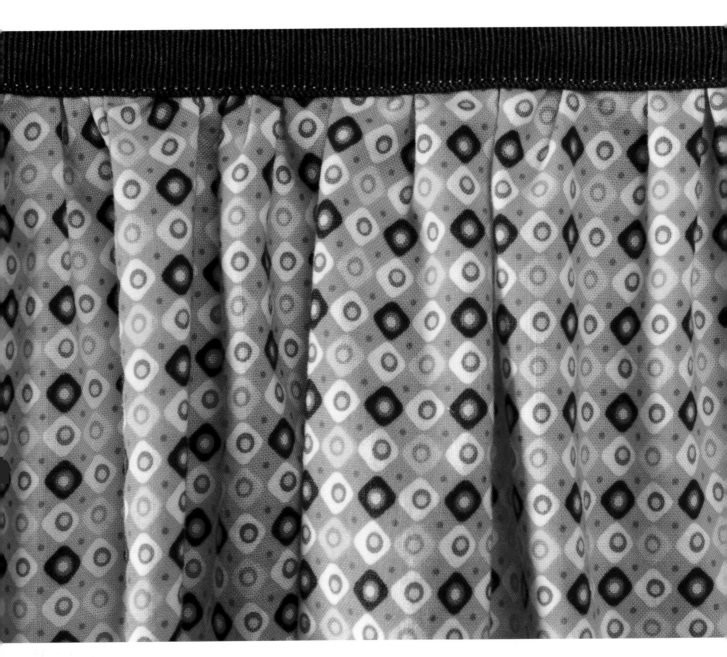

Use a different gathering method depending on the amount of fabric to be gathered.

to gather a small area:

1. Working from the right side, machine stitch two rows of basting ¾″ and ½″ from the edge using an approximately 4 mm-long stitch. Leave long thread tails at each end.

2. Gather the edge to the desired length by pulling the bobbin threads with one hand while evenly distributing the fullness with the other hand.

3. Secure the basting threads at each end by wrapping the thread ends in a figure eight around a pin placed perpendicular to the seamline (**A**).

4. To secure the gathers, stitch ⅝″ from the edge, in between the gathering stitching rows, keeping the gathers smooth and evenly distributed. Stitch again ⅜″ from the edge. Remove the basting thread that's visible from the right side.

to gather a large area:

When gathering yards of fabric, such as gathering an edge for a dust ruffle, use this method, which eliminates the possibility of the basting thread breaking.

1. Working on the fabric wrong side, place a length of lightweight string or narrow cord just inside the seamline of the edge to be gathered.

2. Stitching within the seam allowance and being careful not to catch the string in the stitching, zigzag over the string (**B**).

3. Pull the string to gather the edge and secure the string using the figure-eight method.

4. Stitch the gathers in place on either side of the zigzag stitching. Remove the string to eliminate bulk (the zigzag stitching won't show and doesn't need to be removed).

Use the first gathering method for lightweight fabrics and the second for heavy/stiff fabrics.

A Wrap threads around pins in a figure 8.

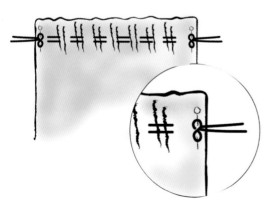

B Zigzag over string just inside seamline.

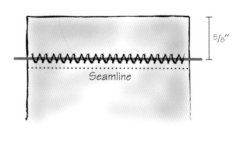

⅝″

Seamline

machine quilting

QUILTING IS USED TO HOLD FABRIC LAYERS TOGETHER. It's most commonly used for quilts, but you can quilt other projects as well, such as place mats, clothing and more. Quilting was orginally done by hand but it can also be done by machine. It can be functional and/or decorative, depending on the look you want to achieve. This article covers just the very basics of machine quilting and details three different stitching techniques.

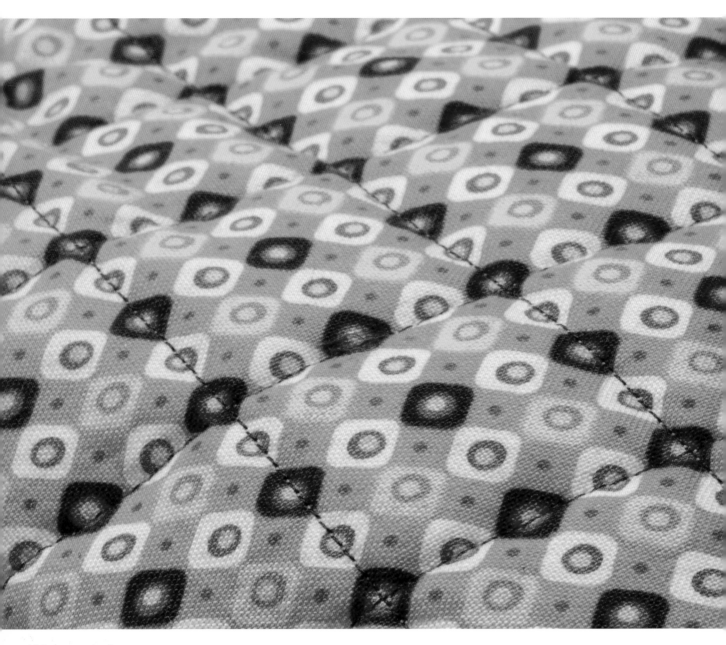

layer the fabric

Quilts usually have three layers—backing, batting and the quilt top. Some projects have only two layers consisting of the backing and the top. In general, the backing should measure approximately 4″ larger than the quilt top. The process of layering the fabric is often referred to as creating the quilt sandwich.

1. Place the backing wrong side up on a hard, smooth surface. Place tape about every 4″ along the edges, stretching the fabric slightly so it's taut and wrinkle-free but not stretched off grain or out of shape (**A**).

2. Smooth the batting over the backing. (If you're not using batting, skip this step.)

3. Center the quilt top right side up over the previous layer(s) (or backing, if you're not using batting).

4. Baste the layers together with thread or secure with safety pins spaced about 6″ apart (**B**). Don't pin over seamlines that you'll be stitching over.

5. Remove the tape from the backing edges.

quilt the project

1. Thread the machine as directed for the project. Set the stitch length for 3 mm.

2. If your machine has a walking foot, attach it. If your machine has an even-feed mechanism, engage it.

3. Begin stitching in the center of the project and work your way toward the edges. The layers will shift slightly as you sew. This method allows the fullness of the layers to be dispersed at the edges, reducing the chance of creating tucks in the fabric. Remove pins as you come to them if necessary.

A Tape backing.

B Baste layers with safety pins.

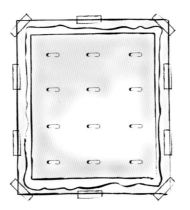

MAKE YOUR MARK

Before marking the quilting lines on your project, test the marker on a fabric scrap. If necessary, test several different markers to find out which one works best on your fabric and is easily removed.

In general:
• Use a **light-colored marker,** such as white or yellow, **to mark dark fabrics.**
• Use a **dark-colored marker,** such as pink or blue, **to mark light fabrics.**

To mark continuous lines, your best bet is to use marking chalk that comes as powder in a rolling wheel dispenser. The roller lets you make even lines that are easily erased from most fabrics. Chalk is available in light and dark colors.

4. Quilt your project using one of the following methods:

Stitch in the ditch—follow the seamlines, stitching with the needle in the well of the seam (**C**). Backstitch at the beginning and end of each line of stitching.

Channel quilting—stitch parallel rows of straight lines going in one direction across the project (**D**). Mark the lines on your project using chalk, an air-soluble marking pen or lengths of tape. Or you can eyeball the distance between the rows for a more irregular effect.

Grid quilting—stitch parallel rows of straight lines in one direction across the project. As with channel quilting, mark the lines on your project using chalk, an air-soluble marking pen or tape, or eyeball the distance. Stitch parallel rows of straight lines in the opposite direction to form a grid (**E**).

C Stitch in the ditch.

D Channel Quilting

E Grid Quilting

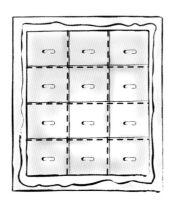

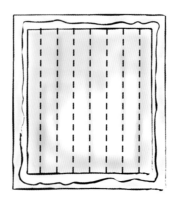

double-fold binding

BINDING IS A STRIP OF FABRIC that folds over the outside raw edges of a multi-layered project for a nice finish. You'll find it used on quilts, clothing and home-décor projects.

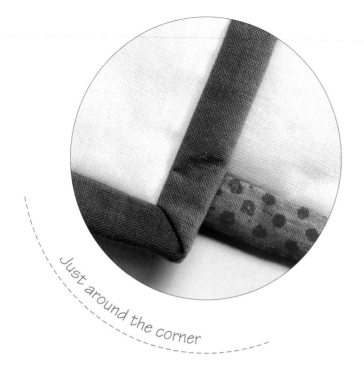

Just around the corner

1. Measure around all the edges of the project that will be covered by the binding. Divide the total inches by 37 to determine the number of strips to cut. Cut strips 2½" wide across the grain of the fabric (from selvage to selvage, the width of the fabric).

2. To join the strips, place the ends of two binding strips perpendicular to each other, right sides together. Stitch diagonally and trim the seam allowances to ¼" (**A**). Join all the strips in this way and press the seam allowances open.

3. Cut one end of the binding strip at a 45° angle. Fold the end ¼" to the wrong side; press.

4. Fold the binding strip in half lengthwise with wrong sides together and raw edges even; press (**B**).

5. Working on the project right side, pin the angle-cut end of the binding near the center of one side with the raw edges even. Begin stitching 4" from the angled end using a ¼" seam allow-

A Stitch and trim binding.

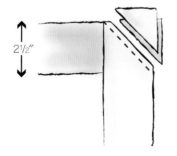

2½"

B Fold and press binding strip.

ance. Stop stitching ¼″ from the edge at the corner; backstitch. Remove the needle from the project and cut the threads.

6. Fold the binding up, and then back down on itself, creating a fold that is even with the upper edge. Align the binding raw edges with the next side. Using a ¼″ seam allowance, stitch from the folded edge (backstitching to secure) to ¼″ from the next corner (**C**). Repeat for all corners.

7. As you reach the beginning point of the binding, cut off any excess length, leaving enough to tuck inside the fold. Hand stitch the ends of the binding along the folded edge using a blind stitch. Pin the ends in place and complete the stitching (**D**).

8. Press the binding toward the seam allowance, and then wrap it over the edge to the back of the project. Pin the binding in place, just covering the machine stitching.

9. Blind stitch the binding to the backing (**E**).

Add unexpected pop by using binding in a bright contrast color or print.

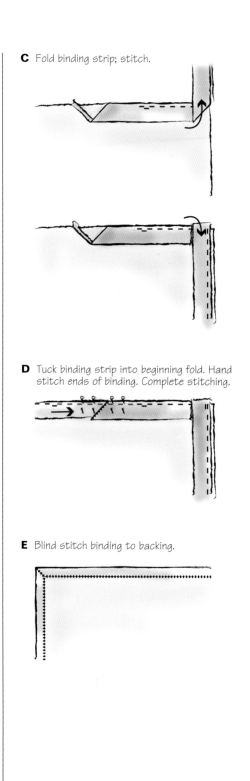

C Fold binding strip; stitch.

D Tuck binding strip into beginning fold. Hand stitch ends of binding. Complete stitching.

E Blind stitch binding to backing.

patch pockets

AS THE NAME SUGGESTS, A PATCH POCKET is attached to the fabric surface like a patch. This pocket can be functional or decorative and can be added to a variety of projects, such as totes, garments or curtains.

pocket with square corners

1. Cut out the pocket using the provided pattern, or cut it the size indicated in the instructions. Transfer any markings, such as foldlines and seamlines, from the pattern to the wrong side of the pocket.

2. Finish the upper edge by folding it under ¼″ to the wrong side; stitch close to the raw edge (**A**).

3. Fold the upper pocket edge to the right side along the foldline; pin in place. Stitch the sides of the fold, backstitching at the beginning and end of each seam. Trim the corners to reduce bulk (**B**). Turn the pocket facing to the wrong side and press the fold.

4. On the wrong side, fold up the lower edge on the seamline; press. Fold in the side edges on the seamlines; press.

5. Working from the right side, edgestitch the facing (**C**).

6. Position the pocket on the project. Stitch the pocket in place around the side and bottom edges. Use short stitches, and sew close to the folded edge. Reinforce the upper corners with straight or triangular stitching (**D** on page 192). Pull the thread ends to the wrong side, tie off and trim.

pocket with round corners

The biggest challenge when making this type of pocket is getting both curves the same. Create a template for perfectly symmetrical pockets every time.

make the template

1. Cut out the pocket pattern on the cutting lines.

2. Cut two 8½″x11″ rectangles from freezer paper. Freezer paper can be used in a copy machine or computer printer to make an accurate template. Be sure the freezer paper isn't curled—it could jam in the printer. Using a scanner or copier, copy the pocket pattern onto the (dull) side of one piece of the freezer paper.

3. To make the template more sturdy, fuse the copy to the second sheet of freezer paper,

A Finish upper edge.

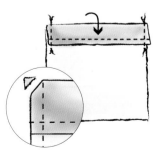

B Stitch sides; trim corners.

C Fold in side and lower edges; edgestitch facing.

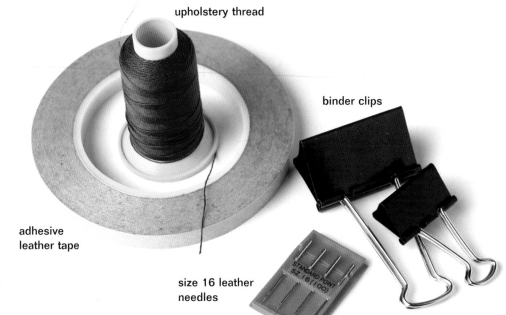

upholstery thread

binder clips

adhesive
leather tape

size 16 leather
needles

1. Fuse interfacing to the leather wrong side (**A**) using the least amount of heat possible and a press cloth. Interfacing helps the leather retain its shape and guides it under the presser foot.

2. Use heavyweight thread, such as topstitching or upholstery thread, and choose a longer stitch length to avoid perforating the leather and tearing it (**B**). Don't backstitch at the beginning or end of a seam; tie off thread tails on the leather wrong side. When topstitching, use a longer stitch length.

3. Don't use pins. Double-sided tape or specialty leather tape (available at macpheeworkshop.com) holds leather without slipping (**C**). And you can reposition hems or seam allowances easily as necessary. Lightweight fabric glues suitable for leather will bond more permanently and won't allow for easy adjustments. Use glue only when you're comfortable and sure you won't need to pull apart pieces.

A Fuse interfacing to leather.

B Use heavy thread and a longer stitch.

C Secure leather with tape.

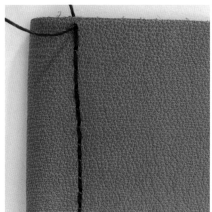

4. Use binder clips instead of pattern weights or pins to secure pattern pieces to the fabric while cutting.

5. DO NOT IRON leather. Finger-press open all seam allowances (**D**). Seam allowances will still gravitate back toward each other, but continued manipulation will help. Apply a small amount of glue between the seam allowance and fabric wrong side using a cotton swab if desired.

6. In thick areas, such as bulky seam allowances or hems, pound the leather slightly using a hammer to make the leather more pliable and flat. Turn the machine wheel by hand when sewing very thick layers. Some leather is too thick for the machine to handle—stick with lightweight cow, lamb and pigskin.

7. Use a new size 16 leather needle. The needle tip creates a clean hole with every stitch.

8. A Teflon foot and soleplate help leather slide through the machine and reduce possible damage to the leather surface. A regular foot and soleplate may be used; however, apply the lightest tension available to avoid crushing or distorting the hide. Adjusting your machine's tension can be tricky depending on the machine. Mark the current setting using tape or a grease pen so you'll be able to set the machine back to "normal" once leather sewing is complete. Consult the machine manual and stitch first on leather scraps to ensure the perfect tension setting.

9. Leave leather edges raw (**E**)—there's no need to serge- or zizag-finish the edges because leather doesn't ravel.

10. Go slow! Until you're completely comfortable with sewing leather, stitch slowly and carefully.

SOURCES | **MacPhee Workshop,** macpheeworkshop.com, provided the adhesive leather tape. | **Prym Consumer USA Inc,** dritz.com, provided the size 16 needles. | **Tandy Leather Factory,** (800) 433-3201, provided the leather samples. Visit tandyleatherfactory.com for ordering information, leathercraft terms, free patterns and sewing tips.

D Finger-press open seams.

E Leave leather edges raw.

fusible appliqué

SPICE UP ANY PROJECT BY ADDING an appliqué. It's a quick and easy way to transform a project from dull to dazzling.

1. When working with fusible web, shapes must be traced in reverse of the finished design. Trace each appliqué shape in reverse to the paper side of the fusible web.

2. Cut out the appliqué shapes just outside of the drawn lines.

3. Fuse the web to the wrong side of the fabric, following the manufacturer's instructions (**A**).

4. Cut out the appliqué shapes on the drawn line; remove the paper.

5. Working on an ironing board, position the appliqués on the project to create the design. The fusible side of the appliqués should be on the right side of the project. Cover with a press cloth; press to fuse in place.

6. Set up the sewing machine for a satin stitch (0.5 mm long, 2.0 mm to 3.0 mm wide). Thread the machine with matching or contrasting thread, depending on the desired effect.

7. Satin stitch around the outer edges of the appliqués (**B**).

To make your projects even more unique, stitch around the appliqués using variegated thread for extra color or metallic thread for a bit of sparkle.

A Fuse shapes to fabric wrong side.

B Satin stitch appliqués in place.

hand embroidery

BASIC HAND EMBROIDERY is proof that you don't need a top-of-the-line sewing machine to create beautifully embellished projects. Armed with simple stitches, you can add charmingly retro-looking accents to projects.

Embroidery floss is made up of six thread strands and is sold by the skein. Remove the paper band holding the skein together and unwind an 18″ length. Separate the strands needed by slowly pulling the strands apart at one end, letting the remainder untwist as you pull.

Instructions are for right-handed sewing. If you're left-handed, reverse them.

lazy daisy

(Use three strands of embroidery floss.)

Bring the needle up through the fabric at 1, down at 2 and up at 3, bringing the needle over the floss. Pull the floss taut. Bring the needle down at 4, making a tiny stitch to anchor the loop.

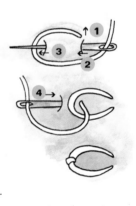

cross-stitch

(Use two strands of embroidery floss.)

Bring the needle up through the fabric at 1, down at 2, up at 3 and down at 4. Pull the floss taut.

running stitch

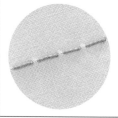

Knot the long end of the thread. Bring the thread up from the wrong side at 1. Insert the needle at 2, up at 3, in at 4 and up at 5. Pull the thread through. Keep the stitches about twice as long as the spaces between them. Knot the thread on the wrong side at the end of the last stitch.

seed stitch

Knot the thread. Take small stitches in random directions to create an irregular dot pattern. Knot the thread on the wrong side at the end of the last stitch.

chain stitch

Knot the thread. Bring the thread up from the wrong side at 1. Make a loop to the left, holding the loop with your left thumb. Insert the needle at 2 and bring it up at 3. Pull the needle and thread through the loop, but not too tightly. Repeat by inserting the needle inside the first loop at 4 and back up at 5. Continue until the entire design line is covered. End by inserting the needle at the bottom of the last stitch; knot the thread on wrong side.

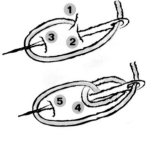

backstitch

Knot the thread. Bring the needle up through the fabric at 1, down at 2 and back up at 3. Repeat as necessary, following the traced line. Knot the thread on the wrong side at the end of the last stitch.

satin stitch

A satin stitch is used to completely fill an area with stitches that are made directly next to each other. Knot the thread. Bring the thread up at 1, down at 2 and up at 3 (which is directly beside 1). Bring the needle down at 4 and up at 5. Keep the stitches within the shape being filled. Knot the thread on the fabric wrong side at the end of the last stitch.

French knot

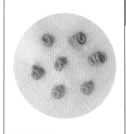

Bring the needle up through the fabric at 1. Holding the floss with your other hand, wrap it around the needle two or three times. Pulling the floss taut with your left hand, insert the needle down at 2, right next to 1. Pull the floss through to the back of the fabric, maintaining the tension on the floss with your left hand until the knot rests on the fabric surface.

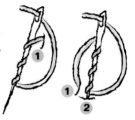

RESOURCES | *Colorful Stitchery* by Kristin Nicholas; Storey Publishing, 2005. | *Creative Crewel Embroidery: Traditions and Innovations* by Judy Jeroy, Lark Books, 1998. | *Crewel Embroidery A Practical Guide* by Shelagh Amor; Sally Milner Publishing, 2002. | *The New Crewel: Exquisite Designs in Contemporary Embroidery* by Katherine Shaughnessy; Sterling Publishing Co., 2005.

yo-yos

MAKING YO-YOS IS A GREAT WAY TO USE UP FABRIC SCRAPS left over from other Sew Simple projects. Originally yo-yos were pieced together to make quilts or appliqués, but these fabric medallions are now used for all sorts of embellishments. Make yo-yos in different sizes and experiment with layering them or adding buttons and beads for extra dimension. Picture their potential uses (a funky pin, jean or jacket trim, a cover for an old purse, a belt, curtains, etc.). Or try the yo-yo scarf on page 100. This is a small project that's done by hand, so you can take several fabric circles with you and stitch up a yo-yo virtually anywhere.

instructions

1. Items you'll need: scrap fabric (twice as large as the finished yo-yo), hand-sewing needle, matching all-purpose thread, compass or round object (twice the finished yo-yo diameter), and a fabric-marking pen or pencil.

2. Determine the size of the finished yo-yo. Multiply that number times two to determine the diameter of the fabric circle. For example, to make a 3"-wide yo-yo, cut a 6"-diameter circle.

3. Use a compass and pencil to draw a circle to the determined size on the fabric wrong side. If you don't have a compass, use a fabric-marking pen to trace a circular object that's the correct size, such as a CD, plate or plastic lid.

4. Cut ¼" outside the drawn circle (**A**). Thread a needle with one strand of thread that's long enough to stitch around the entire circle plus 4". Knot the thread end a few times so the knot won't pop through the fabric.

5. Fold a ½" length of the circle raw edge to the wrong side along the line. Hold the fabric fold with your finger with the wrong side facing you. Insert the needle from the right side and bring it through to the wrong side. Make a few ¼"-long running stitches to secure the fabric (**B**). Fold over another portion of the circle edge and stitch to secure. Work your way around the entire circle. When you reach the original stitching point, end with the needle on the fabric right side.

Yo-yos are even easier to make with the new yo-yo makers from Clover Needlecraft, Inc. These reusable plastic templates give you perfectly spaced stitches, allowing you to create approximately 1³/4" - or 1"-wide yo-yos in no time. Visit clover-usa.com for more information.

A Cut ¼" outside of circle.

B Fold edge to wrong side; stitch.

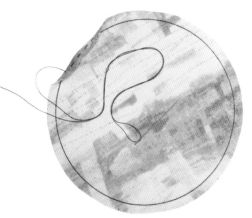

6. Carefully pull the thread to gather the fabric. Work the gathers around the circle to the beginning stitch (**C**). Keep gathering until the stitched circle edge is drawn completely together (for larger yo-yos, there may be a small gap because the gathers are too thick to pull all the way to the center).

7. Take a few stitches in one of the yo-yo gathers to secure the thread. Tie a knot; trim the thread close to the knot. Center the gathers on one side of the yo-yo (**D**). You should have enough thread on the needle to stitch another yo-yo.

8. To stitch yo-yos together, abut two yo-yos with the gathered sides facing. With a needle and knotted thread, make a few small whipstitches through each yo-yo (**E**). Secure the thread with a knot; clip the thread close to the knot. Use coordinating thread for a less visible join.

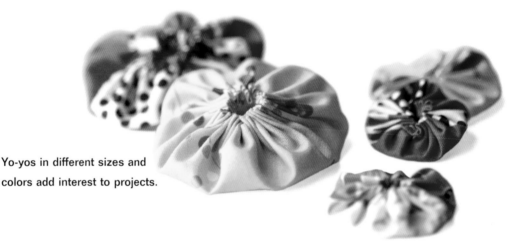

Yo-yos in different sizes and colors add interest to projects.

C Bring gathers to beginning point.

D Center gathers on yo-yo.

E Whipstitch yo-yos together.

making a quilt

QUILTING IS THE PROCESS OF STITCHING TOGETHER THREE FABRIC LAYERS: THE QUILT TOP, THE BATTING AND THE BACKING FABRIC. After that's done, add binding to finish the job. Quilting may seem intimidating, but it's really not—just take it one step at a time.

marking

1. Trace the quilting motif on tracing paper. Place tracing paper under the quilt top with a light source behind. Lightly mark the design on the quilt top with a hard lead pencil or a marker of your choice. Test the marking product for removability before using it on your quilt.

2. Straight lines may be "marked" as you quilt by using masking tape that is pulled away after quilting along its edge.

backing and basting

1. Make the quilt backing 4″ to 8″ larger than the quilt top. Remove the fabric selvages to avoid puckers. Usually 2 or 3 lengths must be sewn together; press the seam allowances open.

2. Place the backing wrong side up on a flat surface, stretch slightly and tape or pin in place.

3. Smooth the batting over the backing.

4. Center the quilt top right side up over the batting.

5. Pin the layers as necessary to secure them while basting.

basting for machine quilting

Machine-quilted tops can be basted with rust-proof safety pins. Begin at the center and place pins 3″ to 4″ apart, avoiding lines to be quilted.

basting for hand quilting

Beginning in the center of the quilt, baste horizontal and vertical lines 4″ to 6″ apart (**A**).

quilting

Quilt in the ditch--refers to quilting right next to the seamline on the side without seam allowances. Outline quilting--refers to quilting ¼″ from the seamline.

machine quilting

Before machine quilting, bring the bobbin thread to the top of the quilt so it doesn't get caught as you quilt: lower the presser foot, hold the top

A Baste horizontal and vertical lines.

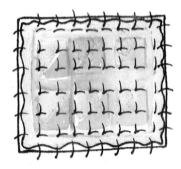

If you need ideas for quilting motifs, visit quiltmaker.com/motifs. Each week they offer a different quilting motif for free.

thread and take one stitch down and up, lift the presser foot to release the thread tension, and tug on the top thread to draw a loop of the bobbin thread to the top of the quilt. Pull the bobbin thread to the top. Lower the needle into the same hole created by the initial stitch, lower the presser foot, and begin quilting.

A walking foot is used for straight-line or ditch quilting. To free-motion quilt, drop (or cover) the feed dogs and use a darning foot. Begin and end the quilting lines with ¼″ of very short stitches to secure.

hand quilting

Hand quilting is done in a short running stitch with a single strand of thread that goes through all three layers.

1. Use a short needle (8 or 9 between) with about 18″ of thread. Make a small knot in the thread.

2. Take a long first stitch (about 1″) through the top and batting only, coming up where the quilting will begin. Tug on the thread to pull the knotted end between the layers.

3. Take short even stitches that are the same size on the top and back of the quilt. Push the needle with a thimble on your middle finger; guide the fabric in front of the needle with the thumb of one hand above the quilt and with the middle finger of your other hand under the quilt (**B**).

4. To end a line of quilting, make a small knot in the thread close to the quilt top, push the needle through the top and batting only and bring it to the surface about 1″ away; tug the thread until the knot pulls through the quilt top, burying the knot in the batting. Clip the thread close to the quilt surface.

binding

1. Baste around the quilt ³⁄₁₆″ from the edges. Trim the batting and backing ¼″ beyond the quilt-top edge.

2. To add a sleeve to the quilt for hanging, see the instructions on page 207.

B Take short, even stitches.   **C** Stitch; trim to ¼″.   **D** Fold binding in half; press.   **E** Fold binding up, then down; stitch.

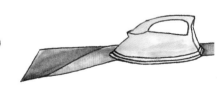

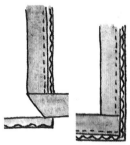

Use contrasting thread to make the quilting pop.

3. To prepare the binding strips, place the ends of two binding strips perpendicular to each other, right sides together. Stitch diagonally and trim to ¼″ (**C**). In this way, join all the strips and press open the seam allowances.

4. Cut the beginning of the binding strip at a 45° angle. Fold the binding strip in half along the length with wrong sides together; press (**D**). Beginning in the middle of a side and leaving a 6″ tail of binding loose, align the binding raw edges with the quilt-top edge.

5. Begin sewing the binding to the quilt using a ¼″ seam allowance. Stop ¼″ from the first corner; backstitch. Remove the needle from the quilt and cut the threads.

6. Fold the binding up, and then back down even with the edge of the quilt. Begin stitching ¼″ from the binding fold, backstitch to secure and continue sewing (**E**). Repeat at all corners.

7. When nearing the starting point, leave at least 12″ of the quilt edge unbound and a 10″ to 12″ binding tail.

8. Smooth the beginning tail over the ending tail. Following the cut edge of the beginning tail, draw a line on the ending tail at a 45° angle (**F**).

9. To add a seam allowance, draw a cutting line ½″ beyond the first line; make sure it guides you to cut the binding tail ½″ longer than the first line (**G**). Cut on this second line (**H**).

10. To join the ends, place them right sides together. Offset the points so the strips match ¼″ in from the edge and sew (**I**). Press the seam allowances open (**J**). Press the section of binding in half and then finish sewing it to the quilt.

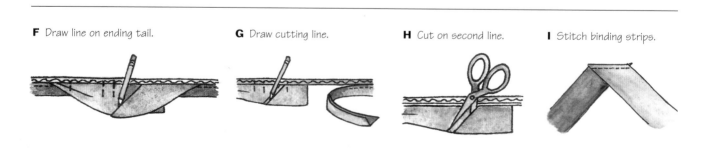

F Draw line on ending tail. **G** Draw cutting line. **H** Cut on second line. **I** Stitch binding strips.

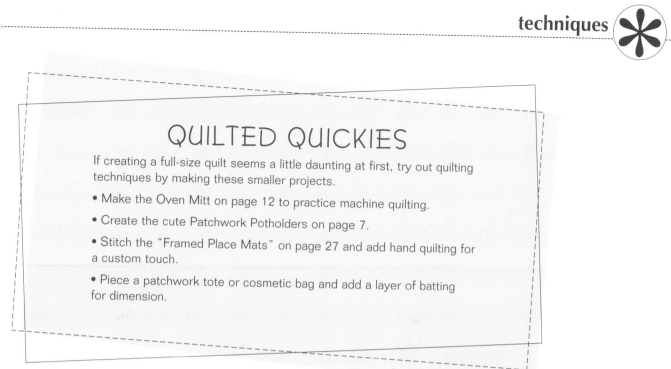

QUILTED QUICKIES

If creating a full-size quilt seems a little daunting at first, try out quilting techniques by making these smaller projects.

- Make the Oven Mitt on page 12 to practice machine quilting.
- Create the cute Patchwork Potholders on page 7.
- Stitch the "Framed Place Mats" on page 27 and add hand quilting for a custom touch.
- Piece a patchwork tote or cosmetic bag and add a layer of batting for dimension.

Trim away the excess backing and batting in the corners only to eliminate bulk.

11. Fold the binding to the back of the quilt, enclosing the extra batting and backing. Blindstitch the binding fold to the backing, just covering the previous line of stitching (**K**).

sleeve for hanging

Sleeve edges can be caught in the seam when you sew the binding to the quilt.

1. Cut the strips listed in the pattern and join for the length needed. Press the seam allowances to one side.

2. Hem the sleeve short ends by folding under ½", pressing, then folding and pressing once more; topstitch close to the hem edge.

3. Fold the sleeve in half lengthwise with wrong sides together; match the raw edges.

4. Center the sleeve on the back and top of the quilt; baste.

5. Sew the binding to the quilt.

6. Once the binding is sewn, smooth the sleeve against the backing and blindstitch along the sleeve lower edge and along the ends, catching some of the batting in the stitches (**L**).

J Press seam allowances open.

K Stitch binding to backing.

L Sew sleeve to backing.

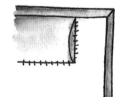

index of techniques and projects